Praise for *Juicy*

Juicy work comes about when work is aesthetic (palate) and pragmatic (nourishing). Sandy brings a keen analytic mind (mathematics background) with eclectic insights, to include somatic as well as cognitive enrichment. Her book is a gift for all of us. Too often career coaching is based on a thin slice, based on this technique or that technique, image consulting or thinly guised psychotherapy. As the title suggests, this book is all about the whole picture, juicy work, something tasty to sink one's teeth into with gusto!

—*Dr. Allan Steinhardt, Vice-President, Booz Allen Hamilton*

As a corporate director who advises rapidly growing companies, I often work directly with management to achieve corporate goals or resolve challenging issues. After reading Juicy Work, I realized I could motivate managers to greater effectiveness by changing my communication: from asserting my opinions to thinking about who they are, what their strengths are, and trying to inspire them to do their best in every situation through using their strengths. The collective impact on these teams has been dramatic, constructive, and positively affected the collaborative efforts in every organization where this was tried.

I subsequently taped a note to my phone with the word **INSPIRE** so I remember to try this any time it's appropriate. My juicy thanks to Sandra Mobley and her book for inspiring me to better myself with my clients—the results were both surprising and immensely satisfying, not to mention the significant positive impact to these people and their organizations.

—*Steve Kirschner, Chairman, Package Perfect*

Juicy Work

Creating Fruitful Careers and Cultivating Nourishing Workplaces

Sandra A. Mobley

-table of contents-

Part III: Finding and Creating an Ideal Environment

-acknowledgements-

I had much support in writing this book and am grateful to many.

Support for my writing journey began with Mary Michael Wagner who taught me to apply my somatic sensibility to my writing. Nancy Shanteau let me talk about my book while she captured the words. Becky Beauman has spent years cleaning up and formatting my work to make it easy for the reader to engage with the concepts. Christine Bruns is someone I have always counted on to take my writing and to make it clear and zippy. Jena Rausch helped make my dream a reality.

My colleagues took the time to read the drafts and offer helpful feedback. They are: Rita Dettore, Margaret Echols, Jane Ferguson, Steve Kirschner, Lisa Marshall, Steve Mobley, Sophia Pallas, and Lori Zukin. My first business partner, Gene Calvert, helped me brainstorm themes for a cover. And Stephanie Katz helped me with a unifying story that linked the pieces together.

I was inspired and supported by Richard Strozzi-Heckler who makes the world juicier for others through innovative practices and beautiful writing. Allan Steinhard looks for the gifts in his staff and helps them have juicy work, and models great leadership. Scott Eblin, who models being a great author, coach and leader, encouraged me to write. Kenneth Kilgore, a leader who sends out daily sayings in English and Spanish, motivates his workforce and creates a company where people can do their juicy work.

My clients amaze me with their courage and openness to change. I have changed their names in the book for anonymity. They trust me with their dreams and let me do my juiciest work with them. They show me that love is possible in the workplace.

I am supported by my Core Individuation community in more ways than I may ever know. My teachers, Desda Zuckerman and Regina Schulman, believed in my potential. My fellow students, especially Rhona Post, Kelly Peters, Sheridan Gates, and Tim DeSutter, kept me in shape to do this creative work.

My coaching group from the Internal Revenue Service encouraged my writing and asked me how I was doing often enough that I dared not finish. Amy Dale, Lynne Feingold, Jack Ferguson, Kevin Holian, and Sally Wright made me want to be a better coach and teacher and to rise to their commitment of being great coaches. My partners in training, Jenn Gillins and Beverly Malone, made the work we did together some of the best work I have ever done because they modeled openness, support, learning and love.

I am grateful to my husband, John Kosut, for encouraging me to take risks and to my sister, Betty Handrick, for always seeing the best in me.

-introduction-

When you hear something described as "juicy," you might think of a luscious piece of fruit, bite into it and it rewards all your senses as it refreshes your spirit and nourishes your body. To be juicy is to be ripe, as in fully mature. To be juicy is also to be tantalizing, as in a bit of sensational gossip. You know something is juicy when you can really sink your teeth into it, literally or figuratively, and when it gets your own juices flowing. Imagine preparing a delicious meal— one so delectable it brings your taste buds alive and is visually appealing, so much so that you *almost* hate to eat it, and it is a meal that feels nourishing to your body and soul, prepared with love and joy.

Juicy work is exactly that. It is work that fulfills and sustains you. It draws on all your strengths and expands abilities you may not even have been aware of. It is work that makes a difference to you and, at its juiciest, a difference to the world.

The purpose of this book is to awaken you to the possibility of bringing all of your energy, passion, knowledge and experience into your career and finding your own juicy work. No matter what your background is or what field you are in, finding juicy work is possible. To attain it, you must recognize what is getting in your way and then, through dialogue and exploration, begin to embody new behaviors, unlock your inner wisdom and creativity, and shape your plan for a juicy work life. My clients have often said, "I want work like you have!" This book is my attempt to make juicy work available to everyone.

Perhaps your work is juicy, but you see other people in your organization struggling. These chapters can help you help others and ultimately create a juicy organization. If you are a leader in your organization you can indeed make the workplace juicier for your employees. Research on the generations entering the workplace now shows that they place a greater emphasis on meaningful work than prior generations. Making your workplace juicier can allow you to attract some of the best talent.

Having spent 15 years searching for a fulfilling career and never losing sight of the possibility, I've discovered that juicy work is possible for everyone. The process of searching for your purpose, how you want to make a difference in the world and find your greatest sense of satisfaction will require you to discover your gifts. I find that people often discount or take their gifts for granted. Once you know your gifts, you can explore where and how their application will bring you the greatest joy and fulfillment. For example, someone may be gifted at selling, but may find fulfillment only in selling something that really matters to them. The person who loves selling houses may not be fulfilled selling insurance products. Once you know what you love, the next steps take you on a journey of discovery to where the world needs the gifts you have to offer. When you can put it all together—combining your gifts, your passion and an environment where you will thrive to provide something the world needs, you will have found a life's work that offers you personal fulfillment and makes a difference in the world. Juicy indeed!

Finding one's strengths or skills is a perennial chapter in self-help books, and certainly it can be a rewarding exercise. But I have found that when it comes to identifying potential juicy work, there is no need to identify every potential strength. Your juicy work will probably relate to your most defining strength, typically a trait that friends and colleagues alike consistently see in you. I have been told my key strength is being able to "cut through a mass of data and create clarity like a laser beam." Laser-beam clarity has many interesting applications. For example, when an organization is restructuring, I am able to sift quickly through the mountains of data and competing points of view to design a workable solution and get buy-in for organizational change. Another useful application of my clarity is in group facilitation. I'm someone who can look at all the data and group dynamics and help the group decide what is important and how to get there. In coaching, I often help people who are struggling with career and life transitions determine where they want to go next. My laser-like clarity is both helpful to others and satisfying to me, and I know it has made a difference. Whether I am working with groups or individuals, I help them stay focused and they reach their goals.

Passion is another self-help staple, but it is not confined to those keep-the-romance-in-your-marriage books. The passion in juicy work relates to the things that make you come alive when you do them. I can be exhausted from a morning filled with conference calls, project work, errands and meetings, but put me in front of a group of leaders who want to learn how to be coaches and I go from flat to fluffy—excited and joyful about what I am doing. For some, the problem is not identifying what you are passionate about, but finding a job that fulfills your passion *and* pays the bills. Too often we feel we must trade passion for salary, but in the long run, that compromise undermines our ability to reach our purpose and goals and to achieve happiness.

Once you have identified your gifts and know your passion, your excitement will likely increase when you work with like-minded people in an environment that supports your values. When you search for where to bring your gifts forward, there will be certain groups for which you have affinity. You might be great at sales, but happier with a group of individuals that has fun together and is focused, for example, on helping people realize their dreams for having a home. You share a vision that goes beyond having a house, to what it means to have a home. As this example shows, juicy work is not just a job selling, it is selling applied to something you are passionate about, in an environment that rewards that passion, so you can make a difference in someone's life and in the world. Juicy work is about finding the right environment in terms of an organization's goals and working with colleagues who bring out the best in you, all the while offering your own greatest good, the highest and best use of your defining strengths, so you can make a difference.

I frequently volunteer at an organization that helps people who have lost their homes and are struggling to get back on their feet. The organization provides groceries, shelter and childcare so that parents can go to work knowing that some of their basic necessities are taken care of. This organization needs volunteers to do grocery shopping and childcare, both activities I can easily do. But a lot of other people can do those things too, and may even take more pleasure from it. On the other hand, not that many people can teach self-esteem, goal-setting, and financial management, so I choose to put my energy there. It is the highest and best use of my skills and gifts, applied to what people need. It makes the work extremely fulfilling, and it makes a difference. This is what I mean by choosing juicy work when applying your gifts. Notice that it may not matter whether you get paid to do your juicy work.

This book is filled with vivid stories of individuals who have embarked on the process of finding their own juicy work. They have agreed to share their struggles and successes in the hopes that their experiences may provide you with a blueprint for starting out on your own journey. Just as individuals can embark on a path to juicy work, so too can organizations. Whether you are an executive who can directly affect the prevailing culture, or an employee choosing where and how to bring your gifts to work, assessing an organization's potential for juicy work can help you become more informed and make more enlightened choices. If you are in a leadership position, you also have the opportunity to leave behind a juicy culture that is your legacy.

In my career, offering juicy work transition coaching, leadership development and somatic bodywork to business and executive leaders, I have been privileged to witness people's entire bodies change as they loosen their subconscious constraints and move toward a future that excites them. One of my favorite examples is a partner in a law firm. Ned was rigid in his stance, speaking, and orientation to work. During our coaching sessions, he determined that his underlying desire was to influence the firm to be more relationship oriented, and he realized that one way to get there was to model that behavior. As he focused on relationships and changed his body posture from rigid to accessible, he built more collaborative work teams and spoke to associates in a more supportive way. His own physical transformation was necessary before he could be part of the change he wanted to make transpire. It signaled to all his coworkers a change in the prevailing culture.

The chapters in this book will guide you through the process of discovering your own juicy work.

Chapter 1: Sweet Spot Analysis

This chapter helps you assess the kind of work you are doing and imagine work that you can do joyfully and effortlessly all day every day.

Chapter 2: How to See Blind Spots

Chapter 2 discusses how to recognize the obstacles getting in the way of attaining juicy work. Once we realize the existence of these blind spots, we can illuminate them and reorient ourselves to examine them head on.

Chapter 3: Gain Without Pain: Who Said Feedback Has to Hurt?

This chapter explores the effects of poorly given feedback and artful ways to do it right. We explore the impact of feedback not just on the individual, but the possibilities of creating a feedback-rich culture that can provide opportunities for growth and learning throughout the organization.

Chapter 4: What's Your Body Saying Behind Your Back?

In Chapter 4, we look at how what you say you want and how you behave when you say it may be at cross-purposes—and what it takes to align the two. This chapter provides tools to help you look at your body language, see what is apparent to others that you may not be aware of, and determine what you want to change.

Chapter 5: The Knowing-Doing Gap

Chapter 5 examines the difference between knowing what you want to do and being able to do it—what I call the "Knowing-Doing Gap"—and how it impacts your ability to find your juicy work. In this chapter, you will learn the tools to help you change the behavior you uncovered in the previous chapter and make shifts in your body language.

Chapter 6: From Drama and Trauma to Building Relationships at Work

Chapter 6 examines behaviors that cause pain in the workplace, where the behaviors come from, and how to address them when they might take more than a little tweak in order to change.

Chapter 7: The Learning Mindset

A learning mindset is always present in people who are doing juicy work. This chapter looks at the elements of a learning mindset and provides the steps to developing this valuable key to creating juicy work and fostering an inspired work environment.

Getting Started

The book in your hands contains stories and exercises that will take you on your own path to finding juicy work or creating a juicy work

Introduction

place. I wish you well on the journey. Often our fears of change are much greater than the experience of it, and, as my clients report to me, they start feeling juicier the minute they get on the path toward juicy work. Juicy work is not only about a destination, but, also the process of getting there. Once you know how to find your strengths, to apply them to your passions, and to identify the right environment to bring them to fruition, you will be able to make transitions throughout your life, each time moving toward your own juicy work.

Sandy Mobley
Falls Church, VA

Part 1

What You Do Matters!

-chapter 1-

Sweet Spot Analysis

"Follow your bliss and the universe will open doors
where there were only walls."
Joseph Campbell

"To love what you do and feel that it matters…
how could anything be more fun?"
Katherine Graham

It was my first meeting with a new client. She was a manager at a big consulting firm and she was very successful. She had been moved to a new job where she was in charge of strategic planning. It was quite a promotion.

I asked her, "How do you feel about your new job?"

She said, "I really hate it. I'm doing all this administrative work, and I am far away from the clients."

I raised my eyebrows, "What *do* you want to do?"

She burst into tears and said, "I want to bake pies, and arrange flowers, and do something creative with my life."

You will see where her story goes at the end of this chapter!

Not every coaching story is so dramatic, but I see a lot of people in my work who are either doing something they do not want to do or doing it in the wrong place. That is when a Sweet Spot Analysis is called for.

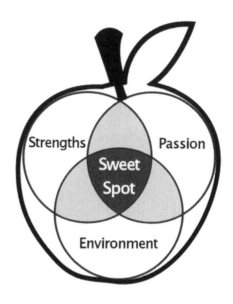

There is a sweet spot where your passions, strengths and the ideal environment overlap, as shown in the Venn diagram above, where the three circles intersect. For example, I am pretty passionate about singing; I really enjoy it but I am not a very skilled singer. On the other hand, I am very skilled as a programmer, but my juices do not get flowing doing that work. In fact, if anything, programming makes me feel drained at the end of the day. I enjoy doing craft projects, but if I am being honest, I would have to admit that the world does not really need my feeble craft skills, and I know there are plenty of people who are much better at it than I. But, I am also reminded that sometimes great artists such as Vincent Van Gogh are not fully appreciated until after their time—the world just did not know right away that it needed their art. This is not to say that my current craft projects will one day hang in a hushed museum. It does remind me, however, that there are geniuses all around us who are unknown even to themselves. I am passionate about leadership and I am skilled at coaching and teaching it. The environment where I will thrive also has to care about leadership. Bringing my sweet spot to life means finding people and organizations where leadership matters. When my skills, passion and environment converge, my work is juicy!

Recognizing Strengths

The first step to finding your juicy work is to recognize your strengths and unique skills. I was working with a woman in the intelligence community who was frustrated that she could not teach her staff how to look at data and see the patterns she saw. We worked for a couple of sessions on how she could break down her process and teach it. Still they did not get it. So I asked her, "Could it be that you're just more gifted in this area, maybe smarter?"

"No, I'm just average," she replied. "Everybody we hire here is smart."

Later she took an IQ test and found out she was in the 99th percentile in pattern recognition. No wonder her staff could not understand data as quickly as she could.

Realizing her true abilities, she made two course corrections in her work. One, she became more appreciative of why her staff could not perform at her skill level and no longer disparaged them. They were not slackers or slow learners after all. Two, she started looking for roles within the organization where her special ability was the core of what was needed on the job. She asked herself, "In which positions is it essential to be able to discern more complex patterns?" She found a group that had long been struggling with the complexity of their data. In short order, she was able to focus on the problem and develop a workable solution. She ended up doing what she loved to do, every day, with people who valued her skill and her contributions to the team.

There is another woman who reads through her email every day; she clears over 300 emails from her inbox! She was dismissive of staff that did not get back to her. When she learned she was in the 99th percentile in organizational skills, she realized she could go into an organization where there were massive amounts of data, structure it, clean it, and in general bring order to chaos in a way that no one else could. And she loved to do it. She had discovered the perfect combination of her skills, passion and the right environment. She is now working as an executive administrator for the number-three person in her organization and never is a meeting missed or a detail dropped.

To find your sweet spot, you have to look at what you already know about yourself. Start with an assessment of your skills. There are several different approaches I recommend. One is to ask five to seven people you work with what they consider your greatest skills, skills that set you apart from others. Another is to go back over any 360-degree feedback you have received and see where you have consistently scored highest. The book *StrengthsFinder 2.0* by Tom Rath has a useful online assessment that lists your strengths and how they are used in your day-to-day work.

For example: According to *StrengthsFinder 2.0*, one of my strengths is "positivity," which is not something you normally see on an assessment tool. What that competency or strength means is that I look for the good in people, organizations and situations. I see glass three-quarters full and recognize how to leverage the strengths of those I am with.

Evoking Passions

The next step in the Sweet Spot Analysis is to figure out what you are passionate about. I generally find that usually the things we did as children are the things we are passionate about. When I was a little kid, what I loved to do the most was get the other kids together and organize games and fun. A lot of my favorite work today is around teambuilding, which involves organizing people around games and fun, with a purpose of bringing their work to the next level.

Another way to determine passions is to look at the things that you cannot help but do. You walk into a hotel room and you cannot help but move things around to be more aesthetically pleasing. Or you go to a friend's house and you see where they should put their chairs, knickknacks and pillows because you have a passion for pulling things together. Or when you go out for a nice meal, you think, "This would be much better with thyme," or, "I wish they'd made this with butternut squash instead of asparagus." Passions are things that are so satisfying within themselves that it does not matter whether anyone else appreciates what you do in your pursuit of them.

If you are looking for a full-time job, ask yourself, "What can I do for eight hours, all day long, tirelessly and joyfully?" For me, the answer was coaching, and even a stay at a luxury resort can leave me cranky when I cannot practice my passion. One of my worst vacations was ten days in Cozumel, Mexico. I read all the books I brought with me and even went to a movie in Spanish. What I really longed to do was talk to people about their dreams and what they loved to do. Because I was not fluent in the language, I could not talk to anyone. I was miserable on the beach after three days!

You know you are not passionate about your work when the salary has to be a certain amount for you to even consider the job; or when you wake up dreading going to work. Or when eight hours feels like a week. Or when you hope you get sick so you do not have to go to work. Or when everybody says you have got a really good job, and yet you feel empty doing it.

Computer programming was awful for me. I can remember saying to myself, "I'm not even thirty, and I can barely get through the day." I expected to love my work, but when it turned out I did not, I went to business school to find the work I was meant to do, to find juicy work. For the seven years I worked in the information technology industry, I succeeded because I was good at helping people adapt to change, but I was bored by the technology. Then I discovered there was a job where I could work in change management, minus the technology. Perfect!

In helping people discover their passions, I ask them to reflect on three significant experiences. As they tell those stories, I tease out their passions. One senior executive told me about working to win a bid on a proposal. Contracts with the government usually do not extend beyond five years and her firm was re-competing for the contract. She was assessing staff and putting them where they related best with the client. Her particular gift was in finding the combination of technical and interpersonal skills that gelled for staff and client, resulting in low staff turnover and high client retention. By recalling that episode, she realized that she was gifted at turning around projects where the staff was not happy and was not serving the client effectively.

A book called *The Passion Test* by Janet and Chris Attwood can help you sort out what you are passionate about. You begin by answering the question, "If I were doing what I loved, I'd be …" You make a list of ten to fifteen items, then compare each to the other until you reduce the list to your top five. You put actions around the top five to make them a reality. The authors posit that if what you are doing currently is not aligned with your passion, then you are probably pursuing a "should do" rather than a "want to do." Furthermore, being sidetracked by the "should do's" may indicate that you do not have the skills right now that are necessary to pursue your passion. So go get them!

Getting the Environment Right

The third part of the Sweet Spot Analysis is integrating your skills and passions into an environment where you will thrive and your gifts will be valued. Finding this intersection is tricky because it is not a linear process. It is more like repeatedly deconstructing a stew to understand the ingredients that create a sum that is greater than the parts. In addition to "positivity," my particular stew also includes visionary skills. I am great at coming up with options and thinking fast on my feet, but

I also I have a wealth of experience in private and public sector organizations. My passion is to help people learn and grow, and to help organizations become places where I would like to work. Despite my degree in mathematics and years in the computer industry, the intersection of my skills and passion turned out to be in the field of leadership development and career coaching. If you have trouble analyzing your own personal stew, it can be very helpful to consult a coach, someone who will help you think through the union of your skills and passions in creative and new ways and suggest areas about which you may not even be aware for further exploration.

Conducting informational interviewing in various fields can also help you identify the right environment. If you think you might like an engineering position in an information technology environment, call a company that sounds interesting and ask to speak with someone who might be willing to volunteer for an informational telephone interview. Limit each interview to only 20 minutes, so you do not impose on people's time. Target your questions so you can be clear about what you are seeking to understand. Informational interviews also can be conducted in a networking situation or even an informal social  gathering. When you find yourself surrounded by people you know little about, break the ice with a question that can help your quest. You can ask: What's the best job you ever had and what did you like about it?

As you start to close in on an option, look for ways to test drive it through volunteer work or internships. If you are considering teaching, you could volunteer at a literacy program or offer a seminar through an organization like the Learning Annex. These days, internships are not just for young people. With the Internet changing so many companies and job descriptions, it is not unusual to see mid-career people picking up new skills through unpaid work.

Exploring Options

The client I described at the beginning of this chapter wanted to arrange flowers, or do something more creative, but she worked in information technology management, which offers few (as in no) flower-arranging opportunities. My first suggestion was that she apprentice with a floral company, which she did for a day or so a month. In exchange for her help, the owner agreed to tell her about the struggles and joys of the work—what the job required beyond an appreciation for flora, color and balance. Karen quickly developed a sense of the risks before she took the leap into becoming a florist. As she worked for the florist, she realized that the fun part of the job for her, making flower arrangements, was only about ten percent of what was needed to be successful. Her skill in information technology and strategy allowed her to help the business owner put in some technology and processes to help her manage her business and track her finances. Karen found that her experience at the big consulting firm was like taking a boot camp for business management. The business owner had a friend in the catering business and asked Karen if she would help her with the business side of things. Karen readily agreed, since catering was another career she had considered. Once again, she traded her business expertise to learn more about the catering business. Karen loved to decorate for parties, plan the menus, and put the guests at ease. Cooking under pressure was harder for her than she had imagined. So now, Karen had real life experience in two of the areas she was considering—becoming a florist and running a catering company.

Neither option gave Karen all that she was looking for, but she found that setting up business processes for small businesses was fun for her. She loved working with entrepreneurs—especially women who did creative work—and she found she was able to help these small companies become more profitable, with little work on her part.

I asked her to consider setting up business operations for small businesses. She agreed that it used her skills in a more creative way than at the large consulting firm and she was passionate about the companies she had worked with so far. She was not sure she could get enough business to pay for her daughter's college tuition. I asked her how her consulting firm knew if it had enough resources. She showed me how she did business planning for the organization. Then the light bulb went off—of course, she could do a business plan for herself!

Karen found that she needed ten to twelve small companies who would let her set up the business operations and run them for her to equal her current salary. She already had two, so over the next six months, she found four more companies. She asked to work part-time for the consulting firm and they agreed. Six months later she had enough business to quit her job at the big consulting firm and go full-time on her own. Two years later, Karen's company was so successful that she hired two other employees. I asked her how she felt about not arranging flowers or baking pies? She said she realized that those were creative outlets that she only enjoyed occasionally but they really did not use all of her strengths. She felt that the creativity of helping small businesses succeed was constantly challenging and more rewarding than she could have imagined.

One company, Vocation Vacation, has taken this idea of exploring dream occupations and mixed it with a vacation. If you have always dreamed of being a chef, for example, for a week you will get to work in a restaurant and try it out for size. What would it be like to be an emcee on a game show, or an extra on a movie set? With Vocation Vacation, you can find out!

The key is to collect a lot of information and a lot of experiences to help you understand where you are going before you make a big career change. For example, you may have always thought that being a flight attendant would be wonderful—they get to travel the world and meet interesting people. Speak with some flight attendants and they will tell you the other half of the story—spending one day in a city before turning around and flying somewhere else, dealing with unruly passengers, and having little control over your schedule. Often we glamorize other people's work, ignoring the not-so glamorous aspects they confront every day.

In my work I usually find it is not that someone is simply looking for greener pastures (as in more money), but that at a fundamental level, their job does not rock their world. They have a longing for something with greater meaning. Since many people trade security for satisfaction, they do not even consider other options.

It is a dog-eat-dog world, we tell ourselves. So we lower our expectations and lose sight of our dreams. We live by the bumper sticker "I owe, I owe, so off to work I go." Work no longer feeds our energies, rather, it saps them. It is a means to an end: food on the table, a roof over our heads, and a few weeks of vacation a year. It does not have to be that way if you are willing to take a hard look at what you really want.

Once people find a job that is closer in alignment to their skills and interests, I encourage them not to stop there but to use it as a stepping-stone to continue to explore what they are looking for. Like Karen, the florist and catering jobs were steps toward success, but it was not until she started doing business operations for small businesses that she really found her juicy work. When I left business school and went into training for Hewlett Packard, it was a good job, but it was not until I was doing leadership training that I felt like I was on the right path. Then, when I found coaching, I was even closer. Each step took me closer to my juicy work. Now I am moving from coaching to somatic coaching. I am always adding more to my skillset. Juicy work is truly a journey, not a destination. That is good news, because the work just keeps getting more interesting!

People Who Made the Shift

Tom, a Quality Manager for a major computer company, was already on his journey to juicy work when I met him. His Sweet Spot Analysis indicated he definitely had the skillset for his dream job. He had an engineering background and was very process-oriented. He loved to research ways to improve processes and quality and he enjoyed teaching others. The environment was a good fit, working with smart people who cared about quality. There were two aspects of his job that he did not like; he managed about forty people and hated it. He felt overwhelmed by the administrative responsibilities. In addition, he dreaded going to conference after conference and making presentations about his company's innovations in quality. For many people, presenting at conferences is an honor, but not to Tom.

With his skills and environment aligned in his job, Tom realized that the passion was missing, and that he had no sense, despite the conference presentations, that his work made a difference. As a result, he found himself getting angry at work. He had put on 30 extra pounds. He was aggravated by the travel, and overall he was just very unhappy. By examining those two areas—his unfulfilled passion and not doing something that mattered in the world—he realized that what he loved the most was research, writing and teaching about quality. Going to conferences, being a manager, and being a senior leader in his organization did not fulfill him in the least. So, he went to the head of the organization and asked if they would create a new unit, Quality Publications and Training, and let him lead it. They agreed!

After helping the company find his replacement, he was able to focus on what he did best and what made him happiest. Now Tom has written several books on quality and has created a training unit that certifies people in quality techniques. His people present at conferences while Tom stays home and conducts research that makes his training the gold standard in the industry.

His quality of life improved, as did his health. He has time to exercise and to enjoy his family, and, he feels he is making an even bigger contribution to his company than he could have in his old role.

During our first ten to fifteen years in the business world, we measure ourselves by our promotions and do not question them. Sooner or later, most of us reach our own internal ceiling. It is then that we have to get creative to keep our work juicy.

Tom had to let go of the belief that he could do it all and even more onerously, that he should be able to do it all. He was being a good corporate citizen, taking on more and more responsibilities in which he had no interest or great skill. He got promoted past his point of satisfaction, and it took a toll on his daily existence. In his new role, Tom adds tremendous value to the organization by writing books and designing training in quality methods. More satisfied and more valuable to the company, Tom achieved his own juicy work.

Another client asked me to help him plot a course to become a partner with his accounting firm. I asked him what he hoped to gain from being partner. "To choose the work I do and have more free time," he responded. Now, in my experience, I have not met many partners in any profession who could choose their work or who had more free time than when they were associates. I asked him what kind of accounting work he was happiest doing. He explained that he really enjoyed working on mergers and acquisitions, bringing together balance sheets to create a better organization. When it came to M&As, people even said he was a miracle worker, he told me with not a little pride in his voice. But in April, when individual and corporate tax returns are due, he said he wanted to shoot himself he hated it so much. That gave me a clear picture of his passions.

Next, I wanted to know why more free time was so important to him. "I have a small plane and I love to fly," he replied. "There's nothing that makes me feel freer or more alive than flying. In order to keep my license, I have to fly a certain number of hours per month. During tax time, I often don't get to fly. With more free time, I can fly my plane, and take my kids up too." Flying with his family obviously gave him immense satisfaction.

Throughout our discussions, he had a clear understanding of what mattered most to him, and he presented a plan to his firm where he would work three days a week exclusively on M&As. The partners at his firm knew they only had about three days' worth of M&A work a week and that because he was their top talent in that area, they could not afford to let him go. He never did become partner, but he is flying more and enjoying work on those days when he is not in the air.

As this story shows, many times we do not ask for what we want. We do not permit ourselves to imagine the possibilities. We settle for what is available, not what we really want. We may think our jobs or our companies are designed to do things certain, set ways, and we have no other options. If this is the way it has always been done, why would they change it for me?

Do not give up. Be courageous. Ask for what you want or look at things differently. Do not deny your dreams just because no one else has restructured a job, declined a partnership or created a new de-partment— or because whatever you are considering seems hard. If you can dream it, you can achieve it, but if you never dream it, you can never realize it. Bringing about your dream requires a mix of persis-tence and surrender—constant striving yet acceptance that even if you do fall short, you will continue the journey. Remember this: it is better to have a big dream and only achieve part of it than a small dream and achieve it all.

So, what dream have you not allowed to surface? If you could re-design your work, how would you do it?

Perhaps you have a clear vision of what you want, but something is keeping you from getting it. In the next chapters we will explore what may be keeping you from having juicy work. Sara's story will help you see how the process works to find your own juicy work.

How it Looks: Sara's Story

Sweet Spot Analysis

When Sara came to me for coaching, she was a sous chef at an expensive five star restaurant that seated 100 in the main area and another 30 at the bar. She had learned a lot from the ex-ecutive chef and felt ready for something new. Many skills are needed to prepare fabulous meals. There is an art and science to consistent food preparation and presentation that includes a thorough knowledge of all of the food groups and where to procure the best ingredients while maintaining appropriate food costs. In addition, she understands the unique blending of flavors and proportions and when to use herbs and spices to enhance a dish. She knows the best cuts of meat and whether to sauté, roast or braise and the freshness and proper handling of fish that will contribute to the dish being its own signature. Being artful in the timing is important so that the finished dish is perfectly cooked and presented at the right temperature. Finally, being an artist so that the plate becomes the canvas for a beautiful presentation like a work of art is equally important.

She is skilled at creating delicious, healthful meals with fresh ingredients. She knows how to make vegetables sing by delicately preparing them with herbs. She is equally skilled in creating meat and fish dishes that are flavorful. Feeling passionate about meal preparation involves all of her – caring deeply for the process and the result of a delicious meal that satisfies the chef as well as her guests. She knows that it is possible to walk into the kitchen and let her creativity reign, feeling joy with the unique tastes that she is able to create. Sara is enthusiastic in the final presentation and plates in a way that displays her artistic talent as well. It is more than the food to her; it is the ambiance, table decoration, presentation, timing, and style that reflect the desire of the guests. She also understands the economics of the business and knows what to pay attention to in order to turn a profit.

She did not, however, feel the restaurant provided exactly the right environment for her. She found that working in a restaurant was not personal enough because she did not have contact with the people for whom she was cooking. She also felt hampered from being as creative as she wanted to be because the executive chef did not like to have much variation in the meals.

For the next several months she and I explored options that

would satisfy her desires and make her work even juicier. She explored becoming the executive chef for other restaurants where she could have more say over the menu, and while she liked that idea, it still did not get her the customer interaction for which she was looking. She considered starting her own restaurant where she could be more visible to customers and realized it would either have to be small or she would have to have a large staff to support her. She even considered starting a catering business and focusing on high-end dinner parties. That was the idea that seemed most exciting, but she realized that catering was different from what she had been doing and she might need more information before she made the change.

Blind Spots

When Sara decided to consider catering, she wanted to learn more about the business before giving up her current job. She went to work for a well-known catering firm on her days off to learn the business. She was given a party to design and cater and was thrilled at being able to let her creativity flourish. Hearing the client talk about her goals for the party and brainstorming with her was fun and satisfying; however, she had difficulty translating her vision to the other catering staff. She made an amazing soup, but her staff could not replicate it. She had not realized how much she improvised when she cooked. In the restaurant, her executive chef had clearly defined each menu item with limited variation.

When she told the staff how to decorate for the party, she was too "big picture" and they missed the mark by a mile. The client wanted the guests to each feel special so Sara suggested individual picture frames for place cards, which could later hold a photo from the party. The client loved the idea, but when Sara's staff brought in the frames, they lacked the uniqueness that Sara had expected. She ended up having to shop for the frames herself. The staff also did not understand her vision for the movie theme and ended up picking movie figures from *Toy Story* and *Madagascar* (animated movies), when Sara and her client had envisioned elegant and dramatic movies featuring Bette Davis and Humphrey Bogart. Again, Sara ended up shopping for posters and other theme elements that she could not seem to translate to the staff.

Difficulty in taking a vision and translating it into specifics was a big blind spot and a huge hurdle for Sara, if she intended to have others implementing her visions. As she reflected with me about the party, she was frustrated that the staff could not "get" her ideas. I asked her if she had ever struggled with this before. She said that in the restaurant there had been some mishaps when she delegated new tasks like ordering vegetables, or setting up for a big party, or implementing a new credit card system. She said she thought she was giving clear directions and when things did not come back as she expected she was stumped about what to do differently. I asked Sara if she had ever asked staff for feedback on how to work with her better. She said the idea had never occurred to her and she was open to it. I gave her some techniques for asking for feedback so she would not sound either defensive or critical. We role-played until she could ask in an open and curious manner. She practiced staying centered and worked on her breathing, realizing that deep breaths helped her stay calm, but she said she only remembered to center when we were together. I realized that I needed to help Sara to do more breathing practices to embody the ability to center.

Feedback
Now that Sara realized her staff had not understood her vision for the party, she asked for feedback on how she could have communicated better. She had the three staff members review the

party, what worked and what did not, and how she could have worked more effectively with them. She worked hard to not be defensive or blaming and they gave her specific suggestions for clearer communication. Their ideas helped her see how she could have communicated the movie theme better, but she was at a loss in learning how to replicate her recipes. Sara did not realize how gifted she was at tasting something and adding just the right amount of spice or an herb to make a difference in the flavor. She did it intuitively and never measured. How was she going to create consistent recipes when the flavor of the food varied and different amounts of spice were needed? When she thought about what went wrong, she had a hard time feeling like it was her fault and more that the staff was inexperienced. She was somewhat put out at the idea of having to be so specific with the staff.

Knowing-Doing Gap

Sara tried to be more specific with the staff, sitting down with them to describe her vision and brainstorming with them about decorations, themes, music, etc. When they did not get what was obvious to her, even after repeated descriptions, her body language showed her frustration. She spoke louder and faster with a critical, angry tone. This made the staff more uncomfortable and afraid to ask follow-up questions, so they continued to miss the mark. Sara knew that when she could center—physically and emotionally—she could slow down enough to communicate effectively, and, she could reduce the stress she was feeling and passing on to others. To help Sara make centering a more natural response, I asked her to set her watch to beep on the hour every hour. Each time the watch beeped, she was to take a deep breath, feel her feet connected to the earth, and do a quick body check to see where she was holding tension. I asked her to do this for a week and then see if it was happening naturally the next week.

She said she did well until Wednesday, and then got stressed again, so she went back to the hourly beep to remind her to center. Anytime we try new behaviors, it takes many repetitions to become automatic.

While describing and collaborating on the vision became easier, Sara found that as much as she wanted to be more specific, she struggled. She just could not understand what her staff was missing. We talked about personality instruments that define preferences for how we behave and to what we pay attention. I asked if I could do a workshop for her and the staff on personality preferences. They readily agreed. As we went through the different areas of the model there was a good blend in all areas except one. Sara realized that she was a big picture thinker and that her staff was detail oriented. This could be good because the staff paid attention to things she might have missed, like making sure the silverware and glassware was spotless. It really made things hard for Sara when she tried to communicate details that were so obvious to her that she thought they would be obvious to the staff. This led her to realize that she had to hire people who were able to get her vision without so many specifics. What a relief she felt at this realization! Trying to translate what was obvious to her was sapping her energy and taking all the juice out of the catering job.

Her other struggle was in staying open to feedback. When clients complained about the food or anything that she had created, she got defensive and started telling them about her cooking expertise and why she was right and they were wrong—not a good approach for retaining clients. I had worked with Sara to be centered from the start of the engagement so that she could be present in our coaching sessions. She was good at centering and recognizing when she was off-center and bringing herself back to center. I asked her if all chefs agreed on well-prepared food.

She acknowledged that there was a wide margin of acceptability among chefs. We worked on her being able to hear feedback about her food as the client's preference, not as criticism of her ability. We practiced by my telling her that I did not like her food, until she could hear it with curiosity and openness instead of defensiveness. While she never liked hearing that she had disappointed the client, she became better at staying open to what she could do to improve the next time. Her behavior left the clients feeling that she was open to doing her best to meet their expectations.

Drama and Trauma

Sara was an only child so she had not grown up having to negotiate for toys or the last piece of pie. Her parents had been similar to Sara in their approach, so Sara had not realized how other people might be very different from her. She struggled with all the negotiation needed as staff, customers and suppliers brought their needs and drama to her workplace. In her restaurant, the executive chef had handled those issues, so she had not needed to develop this skill. In fact, she had often been unaware of the drama going on as she focused on running the restaurant.

Her strategy had been to ignore the issues, but she found that when she did that they tended to blow up. By maintaining her ability to stay centered and seeing her staff in a positive light, she was able to hear their issues. I asked her to get to know each staff member and what they cared about. I especially wanted her to ask what they hoped to learn or gain from working for her. When she had a better sense of their goals and values, and recognized their values were often different from her own, she could respond to them more effectively. We worked on developing her negotiation skills with practice exercises and that helped her with staff and suppliers as well.

Learning Mindset

Sara thought of herself as having a growth mindset as a chef. She had so many menu options and methods for food preparation that it was hard for her staff to replicate her dishes. She realized that she needed to limit her options if she was going to delegate the preparation. In the area of creating ambiance, table decorations, and theme parties, she was a performer. She had a dozen themes that she could easily implement. At times, when none appealed to the client, she was challenged to stay in learning mode and create new possibilities. I asked her what kept her learning about food preparation and she said it was by reading cookbooks and dining at different restaurants; the new ideas just flowed. I suggested she find a similar strategy around the theme parties to engage her creativity.

After working part-time for the catering company, Sara had a better idea of what the work really entailed. It became clear that catering was a much better fit for her than working in a restaurant. Working in a restaurant was not personal enough and she did not have the contact with the people for whom she was cooking. She started her own business, Catering to *You*, which allows her to do what she enjoys: make memorable experiences for clients, hire other chefs with similar skills and passions, and create food that stretches her endless creativity to make unforgettable meals.

Exercises to identify your sweet spot

Identify Strengths
1. Read your old performance appraisals and note what strengths are consistently recognized. As I looked back, I was surprised how often my ability to sift through large amounts of data and find the root of the issue was mentioned.
2. Ask friends and colleagues to identify your top 3-5 strengths.
3. Take the *StrengthsFinder* assessment.
4. Take the *Strong-Campbell Interest Inventory* or other occupational instruments.

Recognize Passions
1. Remember what you did as a child and think about how that applies to what you are doing today. For example, in elementary school two things I loved to do were to teach the younger kids and to help kids solve problems with other kids. Today my most satisfying work is teaching and coaching leaders, especially on communication and interpersonal issues.
2. Take *The Passion Test* at www.thepassiontest.com
3. Write down all the things you feel passionate about without regard for how it applies to a job. After making your list, think about how that could apply to a job.

What's Your Nurturing Environment?
1. Keep a journal and once a day write down the best part of your day and what made it satisfying.
2. Make a list of all of the things that you like at work (some ideas follow, but are not exhaustive)
   a. Characteristics of the best boss
   b. Characteristics of best co-workers - just like me, diverse, combination
   c. Pace of work - slow and steady, fast and energetic, etc.
   d. Amount of interaction with people - frequent, rare, when you choose, etc.
   e. Quality orientation of company - exceptional, perfectionistic, good enough, does not matter, etc.
   f. Product or service based - we make something or we provide services
   g. Reputation of company
   h. Size of company
   i. Entrepreneurial or bureaucratic
   j. Mission of company
   k. Leadership of the organization

Part 2

Setting Yourself Up for Success

-chapter 2-

How to See Blind Spots (and Fix Them)

"Oh what power the gift gives us to see ourselves as others see us!"

Robert Burns

Self-awareness is critical if you are to find, develop, and increase the juiciness of your work, thus the importance of listening to your body. Self-awareness is also about recognizing your impact on others. Seeing ourselves through others' eyes is not always easy, and our vision can be clouded by blinds spots—things we consciously or subconsciously do not want to see. To identify and overcome these blind spots, it is useful to obtain feedback, either directly or through a third party.

Once, I worked with an organization where the leadership was thinking about selling the company. The senior managers were in a state of fear. Instead of managing their people and addressing their concerns, they were busy assessing who could bring in a lot of money. Whoever had the most productive teams, they assumed, would be most secure under the new leadership. They pushed their teams hard to make "stretch" goals. As a result, everything that people loved about working at the company was shunted aside in the single-minded objective to look good financially.

What these managers did not realize was that if leaders do not keep people happy and motivated, there is not a company to sell. In their focus on fear and personal job security, those leaders lost sight of what made the company great.

Another woman I coached craved the approval of her peers and subordinates, but she was constantly giving mixed signals—signals she did not realize were being shared and compared among her team members. She would shower one team member with praise but complain about her to another person. She did not see that her behavior brought about the things she most feared: that her people would not trust her and would think she was a poor manager.

In helping my clients see their blind spots, one technique I employ is 360 degree feedback interviews. I get feedback from my client's peers, direct reports, bosses, and even their customers. During these assessments I often find that some people are very capable with one group but abysmal with another. Some are phenomenal at managing up and meeting the expectations of their superiors, but they do not build trust with their direct reports or peers. Using 360 degree feedback helps my clients see how others see them; by shining a light on their blind spots, it allows them to focus on the areas where they really need change.

People sometimes fear "piling on" in 360 interviews, they think providing negative feedback will hurt the other person or stifle productivity. Actually, it is an opportunity for everyone at all levels to help promote greater productivity and positivity. If the 360 interviews are conducted correctly, everyone wins—the giver and the receiver. I always shape 360 interviews to focus on productive feedback. I elicit support from the person I am interviewing to help my client improve. All of us have great strengths and development areas. In soliciting feedback, I am first looking for what my client does phenomenally well, because people often do not leverage their greatest strengths. When I tell my clients what their peers value most in them, they are often times surprised, and this is a great segue into discerning what they are really good at—and passionate about.

For example, once when I was interviewing a colleague of my client, he gave this feedback: "Frank has the best strategic mind I've ever seen. He can pull together data and see it in an amazing way. What he's not good at is helping people see what he can see. He's too tedious, and he loses people."

I asked the colleague, "What are you good at?"

He replied, "I'm great at presentations. I wish I were half as strategic as Frank."

With that comment, an opportunity presented itself: "Would you be willing to coach Frank on presentations," I asked, "and receive his coaching on your data analysis and strategy skills?"

When I am conducting the 360 degree feedback interviews, I try to identify and create partnerships so that people who work together help each other bring out the best in themselves—and that often means I end up coaching the interviewees during the process. Another peer of Frank's said, "Frank loses us because he gives us too much detail in his presentations."

I asked, "Have you given him that feedback?"

His colleague shifted in his chair. "No, he'll get too upset."

Instead of dismissing his concern and suggesting that Frank was a big boy who could handle receiving his feedback, I realized that Frank's peer was the one who needed support in offering it. "Would you like to role-play giving that feedback so you can build a stronger relationship between the two of you?" I asked. He readily accepted.

We worked on the feedback conversation until the peer felt ready to speak with Frank. At the end of our conversation he described himself as feeling hopeful, and later reported that he had given Frank feedback directly and with great results. He had even gone on to offer feedback to two other members of the team. It had not been easy, he said, but each time, he and his colleagues made improvements and were getting more comfortable offering and accepting feedback.

During another interview, one of Frank's direct reports stated, "I don't get enough feedback from Frank."

I asked him, "Have you made a direct request for feedback from

Frank?"

As silly as it seems, we often forget that none of us is equipped with a crystal ball. If you are not getting what you want from a relationship—be it personal or business-related—ask for it. In helping an organization or even a personal relationship work effectively, it is necessary to clarify what the parties want to work on and to build partnerships for achieving mutual success, not just success for one person.

After discussing strengths and development areas, I ask interviewees, "If this person could change just one thing, what would you have them change?" This question often illuminates the real issue, and it causes people to step away from superficial issues and focus on fundamental ones.

I find that people who have reached the level organizationally and professionally where they seek an executive coach are doing far more things right than wrong. Yet, many organizations seem to pick on every minor weakness. Things that did not matter early on in your career—or were even considered strengths back then—can become derailers as you advance. For example, a junior manager who shows a lot of initiative, is a self-starter, is highly motivated, and tackles projects with zeal would typically be praised. As she moves up, however, she may find herself moving too quickly and not getting adequate buy-in from team members. Her strength then becomes a weakness, as her role in the organization evolves. Likewise, not working well with others may not be nearly as important at the junior level, but the inability to work collaboratively can be a killer at the executive level.

By recognizing and getting clarity on what is important at each new professional level, people can refocus and leverage their strengths in new ways. They realize pretty quickly that leadership is not about the ability to do the work but about directing the work through others. If leaders continue to do the work, people below them will not grow or add enough value. New managers are particularly susceptible to this desire to go backwards, to continue doing what made them successful. That is why when someone who is good at details moves into management, he might become an unrelenting task master, a micromanager who trusts no one to do as good a job as he. A person's strengths can become his worst weaknesses when they become extremes and when he has been placed in a new position without sufficient guidance.

I usually find when interviewing people during 360 reviews that they do not pull out a foot-long list of perceived slights and annoying behaviors. My clients are relieved to learn there are just a couple of things getting in their way. That does not mean they stop worrying. Sometimes they are afraid they will be confronted with something they cannot change. Or, they fret about making others uncomfortable when they ask for feedback.

For some of us, asking for feedback is like trying on a new pair of jeans and asking, "Does my butt look big?" People are wary of answering that question. They do not know if you are sincere in your inquiry and they are concerned about hurting your feelings, especially if those back pockets really do announce an abundant booty.

Feedback needs to be specific and the person needs to be able to do something about it. Sometimes the feedback can be a surprise. A piece of feedback that surprised me is that sometimes I make people uncomfortable because of how fast I see issues. If they do not see it as fast as I do and I have already moved on, they feel inferior. I thought if I saw the issue, everybody else must see it. Feedback taught me to slow down and recognize that people are not being resistant or trying to sabotage me when they hesitate over what I consider a non-issue; they simply do not see what I see.

I admit, it used to irritate me when what was clear to me was not immediately accepted by all and I would take it personally. "Why does that person question my logic? Isn't it obvious?". "Well no, not to him," I finally realized. Being able to put myself in the other person's shoes, understand where he is coming from, and accept that he is doing the best he can allowed me to help others see what I was seeing rather than to be irritated.

The process of going from irritation to empathy was neither easy nor fast. The first change was to notice my reaction when someone did not understand me or see what I saw. Noticing that I was irritated or frustrated was not enough to change my reaction, but it was a start. The next step was to take a deep breath and to say nothing while I tried to let go of my irritation. I made myself count to five (in my head) while I took a deep breath. Stopping my knee jerk reaction to responding was the hardest and the most effective thing I was able to do.

Waiting to respond helped me in two ways. First, I did not make the situation worse by a harsh response. Second, I gave myself time to be curious about what was really going on with me and how the other person might be feeling. As soon as I imagined how frustrating it might be for the other person to not understand, I took the focus off myself and that helped me be calm. I imagined I was my first grade school teacher who was so kind and gentle, willing to explain something as many times as it took for all of us to understand. She made learning easy and ultimately, my goal is to help others learn. Using curiosity allowed me to ask questions to clarify where the other person and I were tracking and where we were not. Because I was no longer triggered, my questions were open and gentle and led us to discover each others' viewpoints. It took longer for me to see my own behavior and change it than it was to recognize issues for my clients. Seeing how difficult it was for me to recognize my issues and change them helped me be a more empathetic coach.

Once there is clarity on what to work on, and we are leveraging strengths as well as addressing development areas, I help my clients define and design exercises in trying on new behaviors. These exercises should feel safe and support them in learning another way of behaving. With a client who had a hard time making a request, I had her try making a request that did not matter, for example, asking for change at the grocery store without buying something. For someone who has trouble saying no, I make somewhat unreasonable requests of them, often adding an emotional appeal. I might say, "I have so much work to do and my family is coming to town but I haven't had a chance to clean anything and your car always looks so nice. Will you wash my car this weekend?" While that request might be easy to turn down, particularly in a coaching environment, I might work in more subtle requests, such as asking my client to bring me lunch the next time we meet or to pick up my dry cleaning. If you are someone who struggles with saying no, it is difficult to say no to someone who matters to you, no matter how outlandish the request. That is why I start with the outlandish and work my clients toward rebuffing the conceivably, but not really, plausible.

For clients struggling to be concise in their speaking and writing, I have them write down what they want to say in as many words as they need to say it. Then I have them reduce the words by half, then by half again, making sure each version still conveys the right meaning. I have clients do this exercise in written form because it is much harder to do verbally. When they come up with the shortest possible version, we compare it to the original to see where the flab was hiding and then they say aloud what they have written.

When I ask clients to practice these exercises, I also ask them to notice what they are feeling, because often it is that feeling that has been preventing them from changing a behavior. "When I say no to a request, I feel rude or I feel like I'm letting people down," a client might say. Or, "When I shorten my description to one or two sentences, I feel like I'm being unclear, that I won't be giving enough information for others to make a good decision." Rather than allowing those feelings to get in the way of the new behavior, I ask my client, "Given your feeling, what could you do to find out whether you sounded rude (or unclear)?"

The client's eyes brighten. "Well, I could ask, was I clear enough? Or, when I say no, I can ask the person, "How did you feel when I said no to you?"

In learning, we try new behaviors, feel the feelings, and then see if the emotions are real or if we are just imagining them. "If I say no," a client once explained to me, "my employees will feel I'm not there for them." Is that a real or imagined emotion? There is one sure way for her to find out, and that is by asking.

"Did my 'no' make you feel like you can't count on me for support?" she might ask. If the team member says "yes," my client might need to provide justification for her answer. She should not take the team member's response necessarily as a reason to change her answer.

Checking our internal notions of what has happened in an interaction with someone can clarify our understanding and help us to change how we respond going forward. It is important to respond to what is actually happening, rather than to our idea of what is happening. This type of analysis can produce rapid acceleration in the change process.

For some people, even minor behavior changes can feel like monumental transformations to be accompanied by dramatic orchestration: Dun dun ta DUNNN! In fact, most changes are accomplished incrementally and rarely cause a stir. Many times, I will end up working with someone who has trouble pushing back on assignments from the boss. Often a client will tell me that if he pushes back on an assignment, perhaps because the timeframe is unworkable, he is sure his boss will think him unmotivated, incompetent, disrespectful, too assertive, or just lazy. When I have my client check, the boss will often say he respects people who push back, as long as they provide well-reasoned explanations.

Sometimes what your boss is thinking and what you think your boss is thinking are two entirely different things. One of the best ways to find out what your boss is thinking is to ask.

All too often, we agonize over actions that other people barely notice. We think our new behaviors are like a pair of antlers on our heads, attracting undue attention and giving others a reason to question our judgment. Saying no to a request may be new to you, but it is likely others have said it without being judged harshly, if at all. We operate too much based on what is in our heads. I encourage people to get out of their heads and *have conversations with people.*

Feedback—especially feedback designed to help overcome blind spots—should not be a once-a-year ordeal, it should be ongoing. Questions like, "So how's this process working for you?" get you into the feedback conversation and create a dialogue about what works and does not work. When these casual conversations are ongoing, the annual written appraisals reflect continuous progress and are no longer feared as a stink bomb of bad news. As I coach my clients in regular, ongoing conversations, I tell them what is working for me and equally what is not working. That is the model for good relationships.

Because it is easy for people to say what works and what does not work for them, it leaves out the emotional aspect and circumvents a lot of drama. "What's the matter, can't you tell time?" is not likely to get a latecomer to be punctual even if it is said in a joking manner. He might smile, but inwardly he could be fuming: "How dare she imply that I'm stupid! I'm the smartest tech person on the team! She's never liked me." Instead, focus on explaining how a different behavior would work for you. The first time someone comes late to a meeting, you might say afterwards, "By the way, everyone's got tight schedules, so it's really important that we start these meetings on time." When you make a simple, reasonable statement, most people will respond professionally.

Imagine that weeks and weeks go by without that simple request being made. The employee keeps coming late until one day you have had enough and you let loose on the guy. He is shocked and angry. To him, the criticism came out of the blue: "I never knew it was an issue." It has been eating at you ever since the first time he was late, even though you never communicated your standards clearly. "Not that I should have to, he's a professional!" you think, once again counting on those crystal balls everyone is supposed to be equipped with, and now the drama is in full swing.

A Chief Executive Officer (CEO) I worked with wanted to schedule meetings with the top 35 high-potential employees in his organization, but he was overwhelmed at the thought of having to make so many phone calls to set up the appointments. He considered taking them to lunch, but the idea of making reservations and taking so much time for lunch felt onerous. I asked, "Why don't you have your admin call and set it up, have lunch menus, pick what you want, meet at your conference table, and you have an hour and a half of connection time."

He said, "I never wanted to be one of those officious executives. How would people feel if I didn't call myself?" I replied, "If I were in their position, I would be so happy that the president wanted to have lunch with me, that I wouldn't care who called."

This CEO had created an obstacle for himself that seemed insurmountable, and it was keeping him from making a direct connection with his most important employees. By reframing his options and focusing on what was important, he was able to make a difference in the lives of 35 employees, reap a reward for his organization that was immeasurable, and make his company juicier.

Sometimes people do not recognize that the action they are taking produces a different result than they are intending. If no one gives them feedback, they do not learn. The best way to see through blind spots is to ask for feedback. We will talk more about feedback in the next chapter.

Exercises for identifying and
dealing with blind spots:

1. Take assessments to get 360 degree feedback. Notice where your responses are either higher or lower than other respondents.
2. Read past performance appraisals and look for themes.
3. Practice taking deep breaths and meditating; both help you become more centered and better able to handle difficult conversations in the moment.
4. Play a game with yourself when someone seems particularly irritating. Imagine what might be going on for that person that would cause that behavior. While your mind is busy imagining, two good things happen: you have a better appreciation for his or her frame of mind and that allows you to not take the behavior personally.
5. Try safe exercises. As you become successful, try harder ones.
6. Gain clarity on what you want to work.
7. Have the courage to try something new, just like the CEO with his lunch meetings.

-chapter 3-

Gain Without Pain: Who Said Feedback Has to Hurt?

"Mistakes are the usual bridge between inexperience and wisdom."

Phyllis Theroux, essayist, columnist, author

To create juicy work, we need feedback to help us recognize and leverage our strengths, take corrective action, and continue to learn and grow. Imagine driving without a gas gauge or a speedometer. How would you know if you were driving too slowly or speeding? How would you know when you needed gas without running out of fuel or stopping more often than needed to re-fuel? Working in organizations without getting feedback can keep us from reaching our goals. Offering feedback to co-workers and staff can help them see their gifts and recognize ways to improve. Giving feedback creates a work place dedicated to celebrating gifts and looking for ways to get better. Finding ways to ask for feedback can illuminate blind spots before they cause problems.

Organizations tout the merits of managers providing feedback to employees. Human Resource programs offer tools to ensure feedback happens, whether through annual performance evaluations, 360 degree assessments, or management review of employees' work products. As much as the procedures and forms are designed to facilitate meaningful conversations, few managers and even fewer employees are happy with them. In a juicy workplace, feedback would be frequent and constructive.

Most employees do not head into work thinking, "How can I screw things up today?" They want to do a good job and are dependent on feedback to succeed. Feedback offered in conjunction with training, support, coaching, and development encourages people to learn and grow. While no one likes to hear that his performance is not up to standards, it is better to learn what is not effective and have an opportunity to change than to end up derailed within an organization and not knowing why. Getting feedback can help people recognize that they do not have sufficient skills or the passion to be successful *in that particular job.*

There are ways to both give and receive feedback that can lead to improved individual performance as well as overall operational performance. It is important to recognize the power of good feedback, the pitfalls of ineffective feedback, and the actions you can take both as provider and receiver that will make the feedback process feel less like a trip to the dentist and more like a great exercise class where you feel stretched to your capacity, but not injured.

Poorly Done Feedback Takes a Toll

Good feedback motivates people to change. Bad feedback, including comments that are demeaning, vague, or emotionally charged, can leave a person feeling battered. The employee may realize that his performance is not measuring up, and that feels bad enough, but without concrete examples of what he is doing wrong and what he should be doing instead, the employee feels frustrated and helpless to improve. From there it is a short step to low morale and another short step to reduced productivity.

When I was a training manager for a computer company, I was asked to give a presentation on quality to eight managers from our Japan office when they came to tour our manufacturing sites. I memorized their Japanese names in order to greet them in a personal way. I pronounced each of their names perfectly, but when the time came to introduce them to my boss, I completely blanked on *his* name. I had used up my brainpower remembering their names and could not for the life of me remember the name of the man I worked with every day. After the presentation, my boss called me to his office. I was feeling proud for having learned our visitors' names and giving a good presentation, so when my boss scolded, "How could you forget my name?" I was completely taken aback. I apologized immediately, but he went on for twenty minutes about how embarrassed he felt, how I had not shown him the proper respect, and how small he felt. By the time he finished, *I* felt like the injured party. He never even mentioned any of the things I had done right that day. If he had said, "Sandy, you did a great job making our Japanese managers feel at ease by learning their names." I would have quickly apologized for blanking on his name and shared my strategy to make sure that I did not forget his name again. I would have felt better about him and worked even harder to earn his approval.

Digging for Feedback Gold - In spite of how it is given

Admittedly, feedback can be hard to hear, especially when it is carelessly or even cruelly delivered. If you can get past the negative tone, a valuable nugget of information can sometimes be discovered.

I once worked with a computer company to implement a total quality program in its fiber optics division. After a successful kick-off, the leadership team members set a quality goal, six key performance measures and metrics. When I met with the team a month later to assess progress, they admitted that they had fallen behind, but assured me they were still committed. The following month I returned to discover that still no progress had been made. I was disappointed but surmised I had not adequately communicated the importance of the goals. After invoking the name of the CEO and his public commitment to excellence, I told them, "I expect to see significant progress next month. Quality is critical to the success of the company. We all need to do our part." The managers looked back at me sheepishly and nodded their assent. When the General Manager asked me to stop by his office on my way out, I was expecting him to apologize for his team.

The GM closed the door as I entered his office and sat down. Without as much as one pleasantry, he roared, "Who do you think you are to lecture us about quality? We live and die each day based on the quality of our products and just because we don't use your 'performance measures' doesn't mean we don't care about quality."

I felt my face turn bright red, my voice choked in my throat. I mumbled an apology and slunk out of his office before he could see me cry. I did cry when I told my team what had happened. They consoled me, telling me the GM was wrong and he had a reputation for being gruff. When I heard beyond the tone of his voice to what he was saying, I knew he was right. As painful as the feedback was to receive, it has made all the difference in my success as a coach and consultant. It taught me never to think my goals and processes are more important than the clients, to *ask* before jumping to conclusions, and to work collaboratively with clients and not assume that I know better. Recognizing that people and organizations are often doing the best they can given their unique circumstances helped me understand that I cannot impose my expectations on others. The most powerful realization was that if I define my success by someone else changing, I'm putting undue pressure on both of us.

Yes, the GM's feedback was useful. Not everyone can hear beyond an angry delivery to appreciate the content, so I do not recommend his approach. The gift of his feedback was that he opened a new possibility to me and exposed a blind spot, and without that knowledge my effectiveness was limited. However, battering me with the message could have just as easily have caused me to discount it.

At another point in my career, I made an even bigger mistake and received feedback about it from the Chief Operating Officer of a company at which I was consulting. I had shared some sensitive information while working with a professor from a well-known business school to help our organization find different solutions to internal problems. After the professor met with the COO, I was summoned. The COO started by thanking me for my hard work on the initiative. He said, "I know from our work together that you are passionate about wanting us to be successful, so I understand that in your conversations with the professor, you wanted him to have as much information to help the organization as possible. I want to caution you about what you share with outsiders. We have been burned before. The last time we were too forthcoming about our problems, we ended up the subject of a book." Immediately, I realized what I had done wrong and apologized. The COO said, "Point made. I have every confidence in you and your team." I left his office wiser and committed to working even harder. If he had asked me to walk over hot coals, I would have done so.

I learned immensely from the feedback provided by both the GM and the COO. But my trust and dedication to the COO deepened because of the care he took in delivering the feedback. I asked for feedback from him many more times and learned tremendously from his wisdom. While I might occasionally put on my Hazmat gear and ask the GM for feedback, I felt that the less I had to work with him again, the better.

The power of feedback means some people can find themselves teetering between crushing someone's spirit and heightening their motivation. Because feedback is key to improving performance and because its effectiveness hinges on the way it is delivered, it is vital that people on both the giving and the receiving end take steps to reduce the pain and increase the gain during every feedback session.

Set Yourself Up for Success

Sports teams review their plays in great detail, not to ridicule poor performance but to learn from both the good and the bad. A coach who is afraid to point out problems will not have a winning team. When the goals are clear, feedback becomes easier to give and to take. No linebacker would deny his role in a botched play when he sees it on a videotape, nor would he feel that the coach's feedback is unwarranted, because he wants to achieve the goal of winning just as much as his coach.

In coaching thousands of executives, I have yet to come across a client who did not want to hear how others perceive him or her. In fact, they all hunger for feedback, knowing it will help them determine what changes in their behavior will make them more effective. Without the insight that feedback provides, they might as well be warming the bench. One of the characteristics of high performing teams is that they challenge each other to grow and improve. They know that withholding feedback hurts the individual and the team. Building evaluation and feedback into their team process sets an expectation that reviewing performance is as necessary as defining goals. They celebrate accomplishments that come from challenging themselves and each other, and they all want the feedback to be caring and constructive.

Asking for Feedback

I observe that people are reluctant to give feedback, especially when things are not going well. Being unaware that you are missing the mark can cost you clients, promotions, and even your job. Asking for feedback in ways that make it easy to give it will support this process. At the end of a significant meeting, I ask my boss or client to review the meeting with me. I ask what went well. This is a good way to start the conversation and it builds a positive foundation. Then I ask what could have gone better. I am still making it easy for the boss or client to bring up concerns. I note the suggestions and stay open and curious. Lastly, I ask what I could have done better or done differently to improve the meeting. This brings out clear, precise actions that I can incorporate in future meetings. Later in this chapter, I will share more on how to stay open to feedback.

Sometimes a boss or client may not know what goes into doing the job effectively and they may struggle with providing useful feedback. One supervisor, when asked what went well, said, "You did fine." I did not know how to build on that, so I pushed for more specifics. "As you think about the way we outlined the agenda and moved through the topics, how did that work?" I asked. Again, he had little to add. "Did we hit the right issues and spend the appropriate amount of time on each issue?" I probed further. He had nothing to add. Finally, I asked, "Did I engage the other team members and consider all viewpoints before we made decisions?" He agreed that I had. While I got no additional feedback, I provided him with my thought process and structure for running an effective meeting. When I asked him for feedback after another meeting, he had paid attention to the agenda, timing and team involvement and was more aware of what I was doing.

If you are not getting feedback, ask for it: interview customers, bosses, direct reports, even your spouse and children. With knowledge and intention, we can get better. Be judicious from whom you ask for feedback. Choose astute mentors who are where you want to be or who have a broader perspective. Ask valued peers and create a climate of sharing feedback for the sake of mutual growth. Learn to give and ask for meaningful and caring feedback. Remember the person in your life who saw gifts in you before you did and encouraged you to step up to greatness. Bring that quality into your feedback sessions and watch performance soar.

How to Receive Feedback

How you receive feedback will either encourage people to give it to you or cause them to shy away. The key is how you listen. If your demeanor shows openness and receptivity, it encourages the speaker to continue. If your body language and tone of voice indicate resistance, the speaker will likely stop or curtail his comments. To prepare for a feedback session, take a few deep breaths and remember to stay centered. Learning to center yourself is a key skill that I describe in more detail in Chapter 5. Assume the person giving the feedback has only good intentions. Remember that the feedback says as much about the person giving it and his perspective as it does about you.

Ensure you understand the feedback.

After hearing the feedback, repeat it back ("So what you're saying is...") to verify that you understand what the person is really trying to convey. If detailed examples were not given or you cannot recall doing the behavior, ask for specifics.

Thank the feedback giver

Since feedback is a gift intended to help you improve, you should always thank the person who gives you feedback. After all, it may have required a considerable amount of effort for the person to explain the feedback and it may not have been easy to deliver. Be accountable. If it strikes a chord, tell the person how you intend to change your behavior. You could even ask the reviewer to notice and give you feedback when you show improvement.

Engage others in helping you change

Engage the people who give you constructive feedback in supporting your behavior change. A client of mine spoke to all of the people who had given him feedback during his 360 degree review. He told them what he had taken from their feedback and what he intended to do, and he asked them to help him by pointing out changes in his behavior when they saw them. He committed to being open to other points of view and at the end of each meeting he explicitly asked, "Do you feel like I heard and took in your suggestions?" Behavior change tends to happen well before others recognize it, and our tendency is to notice actions that reinforce the old behavior, not the new one. My client received immediate feedback on his progress by asking this question. He also increased awareness among others of his change.

Empathize with the other person

It takes courage to voice a concern, especially when you do not know how the other person will respond. Give the person credit for caring enough to share the feedback and assume that his intentions are good.

Be open and curious

Avoid being defensive. Explaining why we did something or defending it is often an immediate reaction, but doing so shuts down the feedback giver and causes you to come across as resistant. The result is a double-whammy: not only do you have a behavior that is getting in your way, you are also not open to acknowledging or changing it. Do not attack the person giving you feedback by pointing out his deficits. If you offer your own perspective at the time you are given feedback, some people may feel you did not really hear their feedback. It is better to accept it initially and to spend some time reflecting on the validity of the feedback before you respond.

Staying open is doable and may take some practice. When you practice being centered and breathing deeply often enough to embody that behavior under stress, you can replace the defend/attack behaviors with curiosity. Start by assuming that the person is trying to help you. Imagine that you are a detective, trying to understand what led the person to his conclusion. Ask what he saw, heard or felt that led to his assessment of your behavior. Collecting the data without immediately evaluating the validity of it allows you to fully explore the comments. Pay attention to how your questions are being received. If it feels like the person is getting defensive or having trouble coming up with examples, let it go. You might consider asking others if they have noticed the behaviors that were identified. Notice if you start to feel angry or defensive and breathe deeply to stay calm and open before asking any more questions. If you start to get upset, your questions may sound more confrontational than curious.

Close the conversation by thanking the person for the feedback. Later, you can go back and present your viewpoint. Start the conversation by saying that you have given their feedback a lot of thought. It will let them know that you did not take their feedback lightly.

Assess the validity of the feedback

What if the feedback is completely off base? Perhaps the description of the behavior was correct but the motivation behind it was not. One manager accused me of being arrogant because she asked how we should design a program and I immediately offered an idea. "You always think you know the answer to everything," she snapped. I was taken aback because I thought we were brainstorming and I *did* have *an* answer, though certainly not *the* answer. I verified that I heard her concern and committed to asking for clarification before jumping in with an answer. She seemed mollified. Later that day, I asked her if we could review the situation again and explained my perspective. She was open to hearing it and could see my viewpoint, perhaps in part because I had accepted her earlier feedback.

Remember that people giving feedback are human too, and make mistakes. Do not feel that you have to accept observations and assessments that do not ring true. If you are not aware of the behavior, consider how you can collect your own data to validate what others are seeing. First, check out the feedback with others and be open. Find ways to increase your sensitivity. If the feedback is valid, be accountable, if not, as in the example below, bring it to the other person's attention.

A colleague of one of my clients accused her of taking credit for others' work. My client asked for an example and was told that she presented the work of a subcommittee without giving them credit. She could not remember doing so. She thanked the person for bringing it to her attention and apologized for the oversight. After asking several other people who were at the meeting, they told her she had in fact named and thanked the team, even including their names on the second page of the presentation. She went back to the colleague, showed her the presentation, and recounted what her team members had told her. The colleague apologized and agreed to check her facts before voicing her concerns.

Here is an opportunity for the recipient to explore this further. The information was wrong, but was there something else going on that led the person to feel that she did not give credit to others for their work? Ask the person what may have led to her colleague's perception. Perceptions are formed over time and when you take the time to explore and clarify, you may find there is additional useful information.

Willingness to explore the feedback in an open and curious way can also strengthen the relationship by showing your openness and commitment to change.

When You Are Giving Feedback - 10 Tips for Success

Giving effective feedback is both an art and a skill. We cannot always predict how someone will receive our feedback, but there are ways to help ensure your message will be heard and acted upon accordingly. While the process is somewhat straightforward, the time you take to adjust to each person's situation pays off when their performance improves. Here are some tips for giving powerful, yet supportive and caring, feedback.

1. Ask the person if you may offer some feedback.

It is important that the person getting the feedback be in the right frame of mind to receive it. If he is rushing to complete a deadline or trying to rebound from a difficult customer interaction, he may not be able to hear and process the feedback at that time. Asking him if he has the time and attention to hear feedback offers him the opportunity to assess his readiness for a potentially difficult conversation. Unless you are the person's supervisor, if he says he would not like to hear your feedback, let it go. Unwanted feedback is not likely to be valued or acted on.

2. Provide context for the feedback discussion.

Clarifying overall performance before providing feedback helps to put the person at ease. When she is told that she is doing well and the manager is giving her tips for getting better, the feedback is more eagerly received. Without an overall assessment of performance, an employee may feel the feedback is a message to shape up or be fired. Flooded by her fear of losing her job, her performance may decline. Think of an employee reprimanded for typos in her documents; without understanding her overall performance, she may not know if this is a minor problem she should be aware of or a critical issue that is putting her job at risk.

3. Articulate the person's strengths and look for ways to leverage them.

All too often, people tend to gloss over positive feedback and jump to the developmental areas, perhaps out of some misguided sense of modesty. When this happens, I ask them to slow down, marinate in the praise, and consider how to leverage it. I find that when people maximize their competencies, they are far more effective than if they only work on improving development areas. This is not to say that people should ignore deficiencies. On the contrary, it is important to recognize areas that stand in the way of successful performance.

Ted was a feedback-seeking machine, but he only listened for what he could improve, such as his time-management skills. As a result, he spent longer hours in the office trying to respond to every email and made fewer sales calls, not recognizing that his gift at selling was a key factor in his division's success. By asking him to shift his focus to his strength at selling, he increased corporate earnings by 8 percent and had a significant impact on the company. Improving his time management abilities might make Ted's life easier, but it might not have much impact on the bottom line. Ted, like many people, took his strengths for granted, assuming that if he could bring in sales, so could everyone else, and he believed he needed to focus on shoring up weaker areas.

Being a team player is usually considered a great strength, but one executive vice president I worked with was struggling to meet his own goals while helping his peers. He was admired for his willingness to step in and support the other members of the leadership team, but it came at great personal expense, as he was often the first to arrive at work in the morning and the last to go home at night. To prevent burnout, he had to learn to say no. "You have put in long hours on the last three big initiatives," I reminded him. "Do you think they realize the cost to you for helping them? And, won't they want to help you in return?" I encouraged him to leverage his strong personal connection with his peers, enlisting their support in helping him maintain his focus on the key things he was committed to and asking them to accept it when he could not extend his assistance.

4. Be sure that feedback supports the person's goals.

Before I can give relevant feedback, I need to know the other person's vision or goal. Feedback I solicited about one of my accountant clients indicated he was too narrowly focused and needed to learn other functional areas to be more effective in the organization. His goal was to become an expert in one area of tax. Telling him to broaden his skills would not have helped him get where he wanted to go. Instead, we worked on clarifying his career goals with his management and ensuring they supported his plan to deepen his functional expertise.

Another client's 360 degree feedback indicated some people thought he was not assertive enough in executive meetings. Apparently this comment came from his peers, who tended to compete with one another and were often aggressive in defending their viewpoints. My client's goal was to be chosen to lead the acquisition team when his organization acquired a smaller company. He felt being collaborative would increase his colleagues' trust and ultimately gain their support for him to lead the acquisition. Being too aggressive could damage the relationships he had built. I encouraged him to share that goal with his colleagues and ask for their support. He felt doing so was taking a huge risk because then they might try to undermine him. I asked if that was not happening already. He shared his goal with a peer he had worked with successfully before and got his support. Bolstered by that conversation, he shared his goal with another peer who also agreed to support him. To his surprise, by being **vulnerable** with his peers he gained their support and he successfully led the acquisition because his peers trusted him. He had a know-how about the behavior that was needed to lead the acquisition and while he never became aggressive or combative, he was assertive in asking his peers to support his leadership of the acquisition.

To provide effective feedback, it is important to align yourself with the individual's deeper purpose and not impose your own goals or those other people think the individual should be pursuing. I learned that lesson the hard way from the GM in my total quality facilitation role.

5. Look for the one change that, if made, will have the greatest impact on other areas.

A 360 degree feedback for an executive who was a client of mine indicated he lacked respect for others' time, often showing up late to meetings and missing project deadlines. I ascertained that he was a poor manager of time because he was reluctant to disappoint anyone; he would allow people to come to his office and chat with him as long as they wanted and he had trouble saying no to people's requests. By helping him find polite ways to end conversations and to say no to extra projects, he was able to better manage his time and had no trouble showing up on time and hitting deadlines.

6. Focus on what to *do*, rather than what *not* to do.

Developmental feedback is generally accepted more easily if it is presented in a positive way. Instead of saying, "Don't interrupt others in meetings," I might suggest, "Wait three seconds after the speaker stops talking before you speak." It is easier to *do* something than to *stop* doing something. If a client has a tendency to complain about his management, I ask him to identify what the managers are doing well. This shift in perspective can bring about a shift in behavior, outlook, mood—even morale.

7. Give timely examples of specific behavior.

Providing examples helps people understand and accept the feedback. That is why it is important to provide feedback as close to the incident as possible so the person will recall the situation clearly. A colleague frequently interrupted others on the team when they were presenting ideas. After giving him this feedback, his behavior did not change. When I asked him about it, he said he thought I was exaggerating. So, in our next team meeting, I asked him if he would like a gentle indication when he cut other people off. "Sure," he laughed, "catch me if you can." I gave everyone in the meeting a Koosh ball, a soft, rubbery ball made up of rubber band material, and when he interrupted someone they threw the balls at him. After five hits, he called a truce. Awareness is the first step in helping people change their behavior.

In addition to being timely, feedback is most helpful when it cites a specific behavior or quality. "Try again" is essentially what a boss told me when he read the report I had prepared. Had he been able to provide some examples of what I could do differently, my ability to learn and grow would have increased, and I would not have felt so clueless.

8. Highlight the impact that the person's behavior has on others.

When a person understands the impact that a behavior has on other people, the importance of addressing that behavior hits home. After all, if there is no negative impact to a behavior, why bother going through the difficulty of changing it? I pointed out to my client that starting his sentences with "but" led others to think he was disagreeing with them, or worse, dismissing their comments. He could not believe a little word—really just a verbal tick—could have such a profound impact on people. So, for the next half hour, every time he made a statement I began my response with "but." Finally it dawned on him how dismissive that little "but" sounded and he began to understand why people criticized him for being resistant.

9. Gauge how hard hitting you need to be when giving feedback.

Some people are sensitive and get their feelings hurt easily. Others are so impervious to feedback that you feel like you need a sledgehammer to get through to them. Therefore, it is important to temper your feedback to match the personality of the person you are dealing with. When people seem feedback-resistant, often the best way to get their attention is to have them collect their own data. I sometimes ask clients to audiotape or videotape their meetings or presentations and review them afterwards. When they see and hear the behavior they have been criticized for, they finally accept it.

One of my clients had a hard time accepting that her brilliance was not the only criteria for getting her promoted and that her lack of teamwork could keep her from moving up. No matter how I gave her the feedback, she just did not hear me. She was praised in her 360 degree review for her intelligence, competence, commitment to quality, and customer relations. But her peers said she was nasty, sarcastic, demeaning, and critical. She dismissed their negative comments by saying, "Well if they were top performers, I wouldn't have to criticize them." I asked if she really thought they deserved her contempt. She said no, but added she resents people who she perceives do not work as hard as she does. When I asked her what she thought the impact was of her poor treatment of peers, she downplayed it.

To get her to see things from her peers' point of view, I asked her to imagine she had been awarded the Nobel Prize and would be presented with it at a dinner. She bought an expensive designer suit and Ferragamo shoes, had her hair and make-up done professionally, and wore dazzling jewelry to receive her award. As she walked on stage, people started gagging and covering their noses because she had dog poop on the bottom of her shoes. "That," I said, "is how your criticism of peers is received." Despite her many accomplishments, she ended up smelling bad because of her behavior to others. She never forgot this story and recalled it when she went to meetings with peers. Sometimes, a dramatic illustration or metaphor has more impact than dozens of real-world examples.

10. Give feedback when you can be calm, professional, and caring, and afford that courtesy to the receiver.

Creating a positive atmosphere is key to delivering effective feedback, and the way you conduct yourself plays a big part in conveying the right tone. I always make sure I am centered, relaxed, and intentional about how and why I am giving the feedback. I begin with self-examination of my own motivations. If I am irritated at the person, I ask myself if the feedback is intended to help her improve or to make me feel better. When it is the latter, I stay quiet. If I am angry or upset, my emotions will undoubtedly be revealed in my voice and body language, which may cause the person to become defensive and refuse to accept my feedback.

I was irritated when a colleague who I had brought to my client to co-teach with me made offers to the group of additional services *she* could provide. I felt she was taking advantage of the situation to sell herself when I was perfectly capable of delivering those services myself. I was angry and hurt. After the session, I was so upset I could not even speak to her, much less give feedback. As I drove home and reviewed the situation, I realized that I had never set boundaries or expectations with her about additional work with the client and I also recognized that she was better at up-selling than I was. I had some things to learn. I gave her the feedback in a different way than I would have right after the session. I admitted that my lack of clarity on contracting with her had left us open to misunderstanding and going forward, I asked that she not make offers to my client. She heard my request and acknowledged that it was not appropriate for her to make the offers. The air was cleared and our relationship grew stronger from the conversation.

When preparing for a feedback session, recognize that people are not trying to mess up—we all make mistakes—and that feedback that is considerate of the person's ego and desire to do better is more likely to be accepted. Feedback that leaves people feeling battered or shamed robs them of their self-esteem and deprives them of the resources they need to tackle a task they failed at before. Remember that a juicy workplace is a supportive environment where we share responsibility for helping each other grow and improve.

Exercises for getting feedback:

1. An easy way to ask for feedback is to build it into regular conversations with clients, bosses, co-workers, direct reports, spouses, children, and friends. Asking, "How is our relationship working?" And, "Are there things I could do differently to make the relationship better?"

2. Spend time observing others' reactions to you. Notice when you see a change in their face, voice tone, and body language. Describe what you observed and ask for feedback. For example, "When I asked if I could invite my friend to join us it appeared that you hesitated and your 'yes' sounded forced. How do you feel about my request?"

3. Pay attention to how you feel. We are more intuitive than we realize and our bodies can tell when something is off. Describing that feeling in a neutral way can open a conversation that may prevent a flare-up later.

Exercises for giving feedback:

1. Increase the amount of positive feedback you are giving. Do not wait for project completion; give positive feedback on the person's attitude, progress, attention to detail, etc.

2. Feedback for improvement is received better when good work is also acknowledged. Practice giving the feedback with a neutral 3rd party to make sure it will be received positively.

-chapter 4-

What's Your Body Saying Behind Your Back?

"Who you are speaks so loudly, I can't hear what you're saying."

Ralph Waldo Emerson

L earning to be aware of what our body is communicating and the body language of others may provide clues to what is not working, especially when we feel like we know what our juicy work is and we are in the right environment, but things do not seem to be going our way. Having clear and unambiguous communication helps make the work place juicier. Trust is greater because there are not disconnects in what people say and how they behave.

Do you know that the words you say verbally account for only about 10% of what people process from your message? Your tone and body language convey the bulk of your messages. Your non-verbal behavior may be sabotaging your success or getting in the way of your presenting your best self. Have you ever watched someone talking and immediately knew he was not telling the whole truth? It could be overt, like a colleague shaking his head from side to side while saying, "Yes." It could be harder to put a finger on, like your boss averting his eyes while saying, "This merger will be good for both companies." Although you cannot pinpoint anything specific, sometimes the words just do not ring true.

Communication between humans is complex, subliminal, multi-layered. Just as body language alone cannot tell you everything, neither can words alone. By varying the tone and tempo of your voice, you could express the statement "you got the job" with joy, sarcasm, anger, disbelief, or no emotion at all—and you could do it all with or without crossing your arms.

We all have to be taught to be aware of body language, and to read it correctly. The introductory books on the subject say if someone crosses her arms, she is closed or defensive—but perhaps she is cold or feels more comfortable with her arms crossed. There may be much more to her story than this one-dimensional interpretation, and it can be understood only by accounting for emotions and words in addition to body language.

Suppose you want to get promoted. You have done the work, developed the skills, but something is holding you back. You think you are as skilled as others, you feel confident, you want the promotion, and you have told your leadership that you want more responsibility, but still, you get passed over. Checking the way your body is aligned may provide information on what is really going on.

Diagnosing Alignment Gaps

The field of somatics examines the connections among body, emotions, and language. When all three are aligned, your behavior is visibly authentic. When not aligned, your messages ring false to your audience as well as to your subconscious. Some part of ourselves feels off, even though we cannot identify the cause. Imagine a CEO watching striking workers shut down his plant and announcing to the press through clenched teeth, "It takes more than a strike to upset me." Saying that does little to ease the striker's stress and in fact may aggravate the stress even more, leading to greater mismatches among body, emotion, and language. How can we recognize when our bodies and emotions are aligned with our messages? When they are not in sync, how can we bring them into alignment?

One way to diagnose an alignment gap is to examine how the world responds to you. When you communicate, do people understand? When you make requests, do others take action? Do people want to work for you and with you? Do you feel effective in the world? Your language, emotions, and body are most likely out of alignment if you answered "no" or "sometimes" to this question.

There may be inconsistency, for example, in what you say and how you say it. The man who unconsciously smiles broadly when denying a co-worker's request sends a mixed message, yet he wonders why people do not take his denial seriously. His body is talking louder than his words, and it is contradicting what he says.

If you want to send clear messages, it is important to learn what story your body is telling. After all, while everyone else reads our body language and emotions, we are often in the worst position to see them ourselves.

"She Does Great Work, But . . ."

Laura is a principal at a top-tier consulting firm. I began coaching her when she was *finally* being considered to become a partner. For several years Laura had been told, "You aren't quite ready yet. Be patient." She was growing angry and bewildered that the firm had yet to recognize and reward her talent and experience. When I spoke with the firm's partners, I also had a hard time understanding why her promotion was not "in the bag." She met all the formal criteria—selling a tremendous amount of work, delivering on time and profitably, building a stellar team, developing and promoting her people, and modeling all the organizational success qualities for leadership, integrity, and collaboration. The partners said vaguely that she lacked leadership presence, without providing any specifics. When pushed they finally admitted, "I don't know exactly, but something is off."

I decided to observe Laura's interactions with others to uncover the problems the partners could not explain and she herself could not see.

I asked Laura if I could facilitate one of her planning meetings, and she agreed. We defined the agenda and intended outcomes. The goal of the meeting was to develop a strategy that the whole team agreed on to land a new account. At the beginning of the meeting I was struck by Laura's erect stance, direct eye contact, and athletic build. She appeared confident and polished, with an easy laugh and warm smile that lit up her face. With four peers and six subordinates in attendance, Laura kicked off the session, setting a relaxed and confident tone. She joked and they bantered back. She smoothly transitioned into inviting participants to share what they knew about the target organization, its leaders, market strategy, and competitors. Laura listened attentively to each person. The group members treated each other with respect, waiting for one person to finish before speaking. Next, they brainstormed possible offerings for the organization. As expected, Laura was fast and prolific in generating ideas, and her enthusiasm ignited a creative spark that generated more ideas from other participants. Everything I saw pointed to Laura's exceptional leadership ability.

As the brainstorming options were narrowed, two ideas emerged: Laura's and one of her peers. When the group seemed to favor the peer's idea, Laura explained hers again. That's when I noticed her posture shift. She began to lean forward while holding her chin up and looking down her nose. Her voice became higher and louder and her jaw was tight—not just tight, but locked and loaded. The room grew tense. When one person expressed a concern, she cut him off, reiterating her position. Another person jumped in to support him, but Laura retorted, "If you had bothered to study the data, you'd realize that idea is irrelevant." The team's stimulating creative energy drained away. Participants stared at the table. The room grew silent.

I called for a break in the meeting and pulled Laura aside. "What's going on?" I asked.

She said she was frustrated because their idea wouldn't work—she'd been through it before. "They're just wasting time!" she said.

I reminded her of her goal for the *whole team* to agree on a strategy to win the account. "How are you doing toward that goal?" I asked.

"And, how do you think the team feels about you?"

Laura's eyes narrowed and her jaw was clenched as she looked down her nose. "They just don't get it. But what would I know, I've *only* led thirty successful new client wins," she said sarcastically.

I asked her to recall how the meeting had begun and what she thought about her team members as they plunged into the task. Remembering how enthusiastic and happy she had felt to be working with such a strong group, her eyes softened, her jaw relaxed, and she let out a deep sigh.

It became clear to me what was getting in Laura's way. When she was "up," Laura could take a team from zero to sixty miles an hour in seconds, but when she was "down" or disheartened, she could squash their motivation with a single look. Since she could not see what her team saw, I demonstrated it for her and asked her what she noticed. I squinted my eyes, tightened my jaw, and looked down my nose as I haughtily said, "My idea is based on the experience of thirty wins, let's not waste time with other ideas."

"I come across like that?" she asked. I nodded. She was quiet for a few minutes as she recalled numerous similar situations.

Under normal conditions, Laura was easy to work with and brought out the best in her team. When her ideas were challenged or dismissed, she put others on the defensive or shut them down all together. Because she did not behave this way often, it was hard for people to recognize this pattern, and it left them feeling uneasy when they thought about working with her.

Laura is smart and driven to succeed, so her ideas are rarely rejected. But on those rare occasions when they are, she feels her talents are not being recognized and it feeds her resentment over not being promoted. Her reaction can be quick and vicious—and devastating to her career. Her desire to be acknowledged drives her to be great, but it also holds her back when she does not get the recognition she seeks.

To break this pattern, Laura needed to recognize how she was feeling before she erupted into behavior that put others off. This is where somatic principles can help her identify alignment gaps among her words, emotions, and body language and then adjust her response before making a show-stopping comment.

First she needed to slow down. Because of her high energy and strong influence skills, one wrong move on her part could push the whole team over a cliff. By slowing down enough to examine a situation, she could see the impact she had on others and act accordingly.

Going slower often amounts to paying attention to breathing. When Laura breathed deeply into her body until her breath reached her belly, she felt calmer and more confident. When she was calm, she did not overreact. Because we are not typically conscious about our breathing, I gave Laura exercises on taking timeouts to notice how she was breathing. Recognizing that breathing high in the chest increases anxiety motivated Laura to take deeper breaths, and with that she felt more confident.

Next, we increased her awareness of her feelings. She had mastered the ability to deny them, so noticing them was not easy. I had her check her mood at different times during the day and write down how she was feeling. This gave her greater access to her feelings, but she still needed a productive way to deal with them. I had her practice asking questions that helped her understand the other person's perspective. A senior partner said, "I can't believe it took you so long to get this white paper done." Laura's first reaction was to defend and explain how much time went into the white paper. Her second reaction was to attack and say something like, "Guess it's been a long time since you did any real work and you forgot how long these take." Recognizing that neither would lead to a successful outcome, Laura took a deep breath and asked, "What were your expectations for the white paper?" She learned that he only wanted an overview and the additional detail was not needed. His complaint was not about the quality, but rather, that she had "over-engineered" what he needed. She understood his concern and agreed to get more clarity on the goal for future work products before starting them.

Laura had a strong and loyal team and she enlisted them in helping her recognize when she was coming on too strong. They even started doing a brief centering exercise together before starting their meetings. With her team's assistance and her willingness to change, she was promoted to partner with enthusiastic support.

"You're a Nice Guy, But . . ."

Randy, a senior associate at a technology consulting firm, has a blend of exceptional technical, consulting, and interpersonal skills. He seemed unable to get promoted even though he had been with the organization for six years. There were fewer advancement opportunities because the organization had been downsizing in the last year, and Randy felt his best career move was to look elsewhere. He had no trouble getting interviews, usually ending up among the top two or three candidates, but he was not landing any offers. He asked me to help him with his interviewing skills.

The first thing I noticed when I met Randy was his warm smile and cherubic face; on his 6'2" frame, it was quite disarming. As I studied his stance, I noticed that his posture was hunched and bent over, as if he had been riding in a Mini Cooper for too long. Also, for his size, his handshake seemed anemic.

When we sat down, I saw that he slumped in the chair. I learned that he grew up in an upper-middle class family in Georgia, had gone to prep schools, and had an Ivy League college education. He was married and looking forward to starting a family, so advancing his career was important. Thoughtful and articulate, he had even published several technical articles on computer security. With his slight Southern accent, the best word to describe Randy would be *genteel*.

Randy told me about a recent job interview that had involved six peers and the hiring manager. He said the conversations had gone well; his background seemed to be exactly what they were looking for. He expected to get an offer but was surprised when the manager called and said they had chosen someone else. This was the third time this had happened and he could not understand what he was doing wrong. I asked him whether he had requested any feedback from the manager about his candidacy.

"No," he said, looking at me quizzically. "That never occurred to me. I don't think I'd feel comfortable asking that."

"Why would it be uncomfortable?" I asked.

Randy had been turning his head slightly to the side as we talked, making only brief eye contact. When I asked the last question, he looked completely away and down. "It feels impolite to put them on the spot like that." I asked Randy what requests he had made of his current boss for a promotion or for feedback on why he had not been promoted. He admitted he had only jokingly asked if he would be the company's oldest senior associate.

"Does your boss even really know you want a promotion?" I asked. "Have you made it absolutely clear?"

Randy thought if he worked hard, kept the clients happy, was a good team member, and did not make waves, he would be assured a promotion. I suggested he look at the situation from his boss's point of view. "If you had two equally good employees and one pressed you for promotion and the other did not, which would you promote?"

"I never thought about it that way," Randy admitted, "that my lack of directness may be keeping me from getting promoted." I asked Randy to call the last manager who had not hired him and request feedback. "It may feel uncomfortable," I acknowledged, "but what do you have to lose? He's already turned you down." Randy called him for feedback and could not have been more surprised at what he learned.

"You have strong experience and wonderful interpersonal skills," the hiring manager told him. "We all really liked you. But in our business, customers sometimes push too far and we didn't feel like you would be able to push back. That can cost us time and money when we need to do more than the client is paying for."

That feedback came as a shock to Randy. "In my current job, I have to do just that while keeping strong client relationships," he explained. "I'm good at doing it, so what was it that made him think I couldn't do it?" He added with astonishment, "He thinks I'm a *wimp*." I asked Randy to tell me about a time when he pushed back and to describe exactly what he did.

Randy immediately had an example: "On the last project, the client, Sue, waited until the last minute to give assignments and I always stayed late to do them. Then one day I heard a colleague say he couldn't stay late and she said, 'That's ok, I'll get Randy to do it.' At that point I realized I was being too accommodating and Sue was taking advantage of me."

As he recalled this event, Randy's back became so straight I thought his backbone had turned to steel and his direct eye contact was intense. "What did you say to her?" I asked.

"I said that she should not mistake my affability for weakness. Even though I'm a team player, I'm not a fool. And, you know what, she apologized and never gave me a last-minute assignment again."

I realized that Randy let things go for too long before taking action and that he rarely if ever pushed back as a first response. "What kept you from speaking up before?" I asked.

"Well, it takes a lot to get me angry," he answered, "but once I'm there, I can be tough. I want to be careful not to intimidate people."

I asked him if anyone ever told him that he was overpowering. I expected to hear a story about an early job experience, but instead Randy related a story from childhood that has stayed with him for decades.

"Between my height and my booming voice, I can be a terror," he explained. "As a kid, I used to intimidate my cousins. We played army and I was always the general. I made them eat dirt and I tied them to trees until they cried. One day my father found out. He was angry and said that gentlemen do not use their size or power to intimidate others. I was so ashamed that I had disappointed him."

His father's comment about being a gentleman was solid advice, and Randy clearly had taken it to heart, perhaps to an extreme. I suggested that Randy might be able to use his strength in a non-threatening way when interviewing. Surely his size could convey confidence and control, not just brute power.

For the next few months we worked on improving Randy's handshake, posture and eye contact, calibrating between being a slumped-over doormat and an overbearing military general. During interview role-play scenarios, we fine-tuned his posture to convey confidence and strength, while allowing his charm and genteel nature to show through. In his new job, he displays confidence and is nobody's push-over!

Coaching Can Help

Somatic coaching typically requires several face-to-face sessions to diagnose body-emotion-language misalignment, trace its cause, and develop techniques to bring behavior into alignment. I work with my clients to determine what feelings trigger ineffective behavior, to identify ways to recognize when and how these emotions are set off, and to find more effective ways to express them. For Laura and Randy, the time was well spent. They achieved their immediate goals and found juicy work. They now have an ability to more accurately see and hear themselves as others see and hear them. When you consider that we all have alignment gaps that limit our effectiveness, you gain an even greater appreciation of somatic coaching's power to increase awareness and capacity to change.

If you are not getting the responses from the world that you want, you might want to talk to a somatic coach and find out what your body is saying behind your back. Even when you see what is getting in your way, changing the behaviors of your body may take some work. In the next chapter you will get some tips for change.

Changes Can Have Impact

For Laura's team, her sometimes prickly behavior kept her team on edge and took some of the juice out of the workplace. People want to trust their leaders and feel safe to express ideas that might differ from what the boss says. The boss needs to hear if she is missing key information that might make her idea not work.

Whether you pay attention to your body language or to others' body language, there is data to be mined and much to be gained from creating a more relaxed workplace. We will talk more about how to use somatics to make changes in Chapter 5, and to reduce drama and trauma in Chapter 6.

Exercises to learn what your body knows that you don't

1. Ask trusted friends and/or co-workers for feedback on your voice tone and body language.
2. Audio or videotape yourself in various situations. When you listen to or watch the tape, notice how your voice or body language differs when you are relaxed and when you are stressed.
3. Take *Leadership in Action,* offered by the Strozzi Institute, www.strozziinstitute.com. This course increases your awareness of what your body is communicating and provides practices to be centered and authentic in your communication.
4. Read *The Leadership Dojo* by Richard Strozzi-Hecker and do the practices in the book.
5. Work with a somatic coach who can help you identify alignment gaps.

-chapter 5-

The Knowing-Doing Gap

"The only thing that stands between a person and what they want in life is the will to try it and the faith to believe it is possible."

Rich Devos

In our quest for juicy work, we may have received feedback on some things that are holding us back. We want to change, but somehow we cannot quite get there. To be able to change, it helps to see what is getting in our way.

Juicy work is possible when we feel good about ourselves and are effective. Interpersonal and communication skills are often shaped in childhood. Human beings are conditioned through upbringing and culture to behave in ways that might have served at one time, but are no longer effective. These behaviors are so ingrained that we do not realize we have a choice. For example, I was taught as a child to *not* make direct requests of others. This behavior became so automatic that it occurred whenever I wanted something; I had buried the ability to make direct requests. I can remember being at my aunt's house when I was eight years old, wanting desperately an Eskimo Pie ice cream from her freezer and knowing that I dared not ask for it. I could only make a series of hints. "My throat is burning up," I said, prompting my aunt to offer water. "No," I responded, "water won't do, it needs to be *colder* than water." Perhaps some milk, she suggested. "No, milk won't work, I don't like the taste of it, but that is closer to what I'm looking for." Finally, my aunt asked if I'd like an ice cream. Imagine the inefficiency and waste of time if I used that process at work.

I learned with staff to make powerful requests that left no room for interpretation. By bringing this skill into my conversations with superiors, I realized I would save myself a lot of aggravation and disappointment when they could not decode my veiled requests. Until I became aware of this conditioned response, I could only hint and hope that others would know what I desired and respond positively. Awareness of the behavior had to come first before I could undo the conditioning. A coach can help us recognize the ingrained, habituated responses we cannot see and steer us toward more productive behaviors.

Managers and executives are not disembodied heads, required only to *think* leadership. Without the ability to *act*, leaders cannot motivate others, align behavior, or influence change. Action occurs through the body. Action follows awareness, so it is important to notice to what we are paying attention. For example, if a manager is focusing on keeping his team happy, he may not make requests that he feels are unpopular. On the flip side, if a manager is only concerned with getting the work done and not how others feel about doing the work, he runs the risk of alienating the team.

Understanding the Gap

An amazingly hard lesson to grasp is how often we fail at something we have set out to do. Think about the commitments you have made to keep your desk neat, to return phone calls, to respond to emails in one day, or to get to meetings on time. At one time or another—or another and another—you have probably let those pledges fall by the wayside. Since most of my education had been biased toward cognitive learning, that is, relying on facts and theory to guide understanding, I was shocked to learn in an initial Strozzi Institute leadership course how often *knowing* does not translate into *doing*. In a physical (somatic) exercise designed to model making a request, we were told to walk toward the person we were making a request of with our hand out and touch the person just below the throat with an open palm. With the best of intentions my hand always ended up on the other person's shoulder. I do not have vision problems, and I could walk up to someone and touch them under the throat, but in the context of making a request, I missed every time. That is when I saw my own gap. My body knew something that my mind did not.

For example, many people *know* the importance of making an effective request and can even recite the criteria perfectly. Under pressure or in certain situations, they often fall into old, ineffective patterns. Or they might say the right words, but their tone of voice or body language conveys an undermining message. Seeing this dilemma made me more aware that I need to look for and bridge this gap.

After a somatic exercise, my awareness was raised further as I listened to how I made requests. To staff I said, "Please make sure you include me in that client meeting." But with the boss, the same "request" sounded like, "It would be useful to me to attend client meetings." To effectively design leadership programs, hearing first-hand what clients were looking for was important. I clearly *knew* how to make an effective request yet was not able to *do* so in some situations. This made me curious about what happens in that knowing-doing gap.

I learned that the conditioning that causes one behavior to manifest itself over a more effective behavior has been embodied and become habitual. We do it without thinking. To undo the habit requires awareness, recognizing that the old behavior is getting in the way of what we want or need, and continuous practices to embody the new behavior until it becomes automatic. Unlearning an ineffective behavior can be harder than learning a new approach because the old approach has been so ingrained. Imagine moving to a country where people shake hands by extending their left hand. How long would it take to unlearn our habitual right hand shake? There is probably no emotion attached to a right versus left-hand shake. Layer onto the practice either a positive or negative emotion attached to shaking hands a certain way and the unlearning becomes more difficult.

A key factor for anyone hoping to achieve juicy work is authenticity—alignment between saying and doing. People evaluate their leaders more by what they *do* than what they *say*. Dr. Albert Mehrabian from UCLA studied this behavioral difference. He found that if there was a dissonance between what was said and how that person behaved when a person communicated feelings, the audience judged the person's actual words to have only a 7 percent impact on the believability of the message, while the person's voice and body language had a much higher impact on trusting the message, at 38 percent and 55 percent respectively. Clearly a person's actions and voice, with a total 93 percent impact, carry far more weight than the words a person uses. Suppose a leader tells the workforce about an upcoming merger saying, "I am excited and happy about the possibilities this merger will provide," while he looks down at his shoes and speaks with a flat affect. The employees will quickly pick up on his lack of enthusiasm and will distrust the message.

In his book *The Anatomy of Change*, Richard Strozzi-Heckler writes, "Somatics... defines the body as a functional, living whole rather than as a mechanical structure. Somatics does not see a split between the mind and body but views the soma as a unified expression of all that we think, feel, perceive, and express." Somatic coaches show clients how their body language correlates with often hidden and limited inner feelings, narratives, and mindsets. Specifically designed, somatically based practices allow these internal states to shift, enabling clients to take new actions to achieve their goals. For example, if a man grew up being told that "nice boys" do not brag, he may drop his voice and look away from his peers when asked to talk about his projects in a team meeting. He may have no awareness that hiding his talent is limiting his career progression. Once these behaviors are brought to his attention, he will still need time and somatic practices to keep his voice strong and maintain eye contact when talking about his work.

Getting Centered and Using Somatics

To understand somatics you must be attuned to your own body and what you are feeling. Many people have become anesthetized to feelings and tell themselves—that is, tell their bodies—what they can and cannot feel. A person may be saddened by the death of a relative or the loss of a meaningful job, but may feel compelled to put on a happy face and dismiss that emotion. Another person whose boss yells at her several times a week may say, "Oh, he is under pressure and doesn't really mean it." For both people, their bodies ache nonetheless.

Denying feelings does not ease the pain, it just buries it. Numbing and painful feelings decrease the capacity to experience other feelings—such as joy, fear, contentment and surprise. At the other end of the spectrum, some people can be overloaded by the intensity of their feelings to the point that it becomes intolerable and they boil over in rage or panic. In his book *Working with Emotional Intelligence*, Daniel Goleman refers to this as an amygdala hijack. The amygdala is comprised of two almond shaped parts in the brain that act as sensors to tell the brain when an unsafe situation has arisen. In these situations, the primal part of the brain senses an old and uncomfortable emotion and the person is thrown into one of three basic responses—fight, flight, or freeze. The higher functioning part of the brain is cut off and the behavior that results is seldom pretty.

In one scenario, the Board told a division manager that his division was going to be eliminated in a cost-cutting measure and he was required to let his 300 employees go. He went into a rage about how much his division had done for the company, he criticized his boss, and he insulted two of the Board members. As security escorted him out, he realized that his amygdala hijack had cost him his job and his ability to try to find creative ways to redeploy his staff.

To avoid having to swallow feelings or to be ruled by them, it helps to have a place of safety inside oneself that allows time for choice and greater ranges of possibilities. The first step to finding that internal oasis in the body is to learn what it feels like to be centered. Being centered in your body is like shifting to neutral in a car with a manual transmission. It is the place of flexibility that allows for easy movement in any direction. It is a place where you can access your power, focus on what you care about, and tap into the inner wisdom of your body, feelings, and emotions.

There are times when being centered can mean the difference between life and death. Consider the police officer who has a split second to decide whether the person in the heavy overcoat coming his way is carrying a bomb, a weapon, or something harmless such as a cell phone. Being centered can affect whether you win a negotiation, get a job, or hear what is really bothering your teenager.

To center yourself, pay attention to your breath. Is it low in your belly and moving fully through your body? Bringing your attention to your breath helps you center. Notice your posture. Are you slouched or rigid? If so, sit or stand tall with your weight evenly distributed on each side and from front to back. What about your forehead? Is it wrinkled or relaxed? Notice your eyes. Are they staring fixedly or wide open like a deer in the headlights? Relax your eyes—let them soften and increase your peripheral vision. How about your jaw? Is it held tightly? Are you grinding your teeth? Open your mouth as wide as you can and then relax your jaw. How about your shoulders? Are they pulled up tightly near your ears as you carry the weight of the world? Tighten them more and then relax them, feeling the tension slide away. These are some of the key areas where we hold tension. Tension dilutes the center. If we are feeling tightness or pain, our attention goes to these areas and away from feeling centered.

It may be useful to do a centering practice before meetings, especially meetings occurring in the middle of a busy day. Getting centered allows you to let go of other concerns and to be fully present for the session. The more you can bring your awareness to your stance and sensations, the better. Pay attention to your body. Are your shoulders high? It could mean you are taking on too much responsibility. Notice tightness in the jaw area. This may indicate the need to control things or that you are *chewing* on a difficult problem. How is your eye contact? Do you have a "deer in the headlights" look, an intense stare, a sleepy gaze? What do these things mean to you?

Rather than consult a checklist that says if your body is doing this, it means that, adopt a curious mind and try to analyze what is going on under your skin. I sometimes demonstrate what I see for my clients and ask what that posture or look provokes in them. That tends to give me more insight about what a client is experiencing and they in turn see themselves in a new light.

Another way of centering is having clarity on your purpose and values. In Stephen Covey's book *The 7 Habits of Highly Effective People*, he talks about being principle centered. When you are clear about your values and your purpose, it is easier to make the right decisions. Imagine that you and a co-worker are being considered for a promotion. You are working together on the project and when it is time to brief it to top management, your colleague is home sick. If you are driven to win at all costs, you might not mention your colleague's work in the presentation. If you are principle centered and one of your principles is helping workplaces be juicier for all, you will talk about your colleague's contribution in a positive light, as if he were in the room with you.

How It Works: Somatics in Action

Carol is a senior government official in an important position with the Department of Defense. Before I had met her, I assumed she would be somewhat rigid in her posture, buttoned down and stern. When a slight woman dressed in a flowered blouse and light blue skirt with wispy blonde hair and a shy demeanor met me on our first appointment, I presumed she was Carol's administrative assistant coming to escort me through security. Imagine my surprise when she introduced herself as Carol.

Carol possesses a brilliant mind and is one of only three women to rise above the Director level in that department. I learned that she is an excellent project leader, able to see the big picture while still keeping track of all the details needed to make a project succeed. Possessing strong influencing skills, she would thrive in a more collaborative work environment, but her difficulty making direct requests allowed others to take advantage of her in this competitive workplace. Carol was referred to me because in order to meet her goals, it was essential for her to get other parts of the organization to work together. To do this she had to learn to make requests effectively.

When I asked Carol to show me how she makes requests, the results were fascinating. She blinked her eyes nervously, her mouth twitched, and her posture became slumped. She appeared to be begging. Her language became indirect, prefacing her requests with words like, "I would like it *if* ..." or "We may need ..." or even "I wish..." She told me people would respond to her with nods, but rarely would anyone take action. She was burning out from lack of support.

I asked her to give me examples of assertive people in her organization. She described only men. I asked her to tell me about some assertive females. She said there were two, both of whom she described as aggressive, attacking pit bulls who frequently raised their voices, barked out orders, and never listened. She could not identify a single woman who was assertive in a positive way. In her world, women were either vicious sharks or meek little mice. She felt revulsion at the thought of being a shark.

I began by demonstrating a continuum of behaviors between Mouse and Shark. First I made a request at the Mouse end. I rounded my shoulders, crouched down, looked up through my eyelashes, avoided eye contact and said in a soft voice, "It would be nice, uh, uh, do you think maybe we could finish the project today?" Carol observed that the Mouse-me was so hesitant that it was unclear what I was actually requesting and she felt no urgency to comply. I asked her to match my Mouse posture. She did it easily and said that this stance felt all too familiar.

I then demonstrated the Shark-me. I puffed up my chest and demanded, "I want the completed project on my desk by the end of the day or you can look for work elsewhere." She took a step back, her face froze into a mask, and the light went out in her eyes. I asked her what she experienced and she said she felt afraid. "But," she added in a feisty voice, "if you didn't have the authority, you could hold your breath before I'd respond to a demand phrased like that." I noted that she sounded angry. She agreed and said, "People who abuse their power really infuriate me." I asked her to notice her posture. She was standing tall and making direct eye contact. "This is you stepping into your power," I said, "notice how it feels." I suggested there might be some benefit to harnessing her inner-Shark. "For example, you notice this feeling when someone has stepped over a boundary. Instead of shrinking, you can use the feeling to get in touch with your power and prevent someone from pushing you where you do not want to go."

I then demonstrated a centered, confident, direct request for her. I stood with my feet shoulder width apart, my back straight and aligned with head over shoulders over hips over feet, all in one continuous line. I made direct eye contact. Breathing in a relaxed manner, I spoke in a strong, even voice: "Please have the project on my desk by the end of the day." As I made the request, I noticed that Carol also seemed relaxed. She met my eye contact and her posture shifted from slouched to more erect. She was surprised that I could be so strong without being offensive and she said she felt "invited" to hear my request.

For the rest of the session, I modeled and she practiced moving in small increments along the Mouse-Shark continuum. Sometimes when people make a change, they go too far in the opposite direction. My goal was for Carol to know what degree of directness was appropriate for her. Awareness is the first step toward making a change. At the end of the session, Carol was already making progress towards harnessing assertive behaviors that would enable her to lead effectively, without becoming a pit bull or a shark. We had made good progress.

As we walked toward the elevator, a colleague walked by and called her Cheryl. I asked if her name was Carol or Cheryl. She admitted it was Cheryl. She had let me call her Carol throughout the entire first session because she was embarrassed to correct me!

Cheryl's homework for the next week was to practice making requests in a direct, not indirect, way—like asking her change-resistant secretary to re-do the filing system or asking her coach to call her by her correct name. When we met again, Cheryl had made requests, and, for her, that was a positive step forward. I began by calling her Carol. She quickly asked me to call her Cheryl. As she described successes, it became clear that she had made the most requests of people she thought would be amenable. For the following week, I challenged her to make more difficult requests and to notice her body language and what she was feeling and to make notes for us to discuss at our next session. My goal was to help Cheryl *feel* how to make requests from a centered place and to notice her own and others' responses when she did so. I wanted her to embody making strong requests and not to lapse into her Mouse body, which made requests that were easy to ignore.

At our next meeting, she reported that she had been able to make more challenging requests of her staff, such as asking them to take on more project responsibilities. Most of her difficulty had occurred when asking peers in other departments for help. She recounted many instances when she had helped others with resources, provided support for their proposals, and even times when she shared money from her budget to help fund the projects of others. When she needed assistance, her peers consistently failed to reciprocate. Two things became evident: 1) she never let others know that helping them was a cost to her, so they thought she had excess budget and resources, and 2) she never stated her expectations that they reciprocate. She had set up an expectation of a one-way relationship (she gave, they did not) and they were happy to keep it that way.

Underlying Cheryl's difficulty was her belief that if she did nice things, people would naturally reciprocate. She would not *have* to make requests. I asked her how she would feel making a request of her peers. She said she actually had several requests in mind. Her posture was strong and I could see that she was harnessing her power. She said that she was tired of their ignoring her and never offering help with her projects. I asked her to remember the sensation in her body when someone called her by the wrong name and instead of ignoring the feeling, to use it to get in touch with how irritating it feels to be dismissed and ignored.

Her homework for the next session was to continue making challenging requests and to pay attention to her feelings when she made them.

When we met again we discussed requests she had made to her peers. She reported several successes and one devastating failure. She had asked Tom, notoriously rude and the most alpha male on the team, to loan two people from his department to assist with a project that had a tight deadline. He ignored her and simply walked away. She felt angry and hurt, but rather than bury the feeling, she followed him to his office and made the request again. He did not look away from his computer as he said, "Look, my people are overworked. I can't help you." She did not know what to say then. She felt so low she could have slipped under the door.

I suggested we practice. I role-played Tom and asked her to make a request of me. As direct as Cheryl had been in a previous session when she asked me to call her by her correct name, her posture reverted back to Mouse with resigned body, slumped shoulders and downcast eyes. When I asked her what had caused her stance to change, she said she felt all her emotions pulling her to be indirect. "What emotions?" I asked. "Be specific." "I think … just the pain of being rejected," she said. As a peer, she had no power to reverse his rejection. Tom's "no" represented disrespect and powerlessness and she feared that when he rejected her request she looked even weaker for asking. This was another layer that kept Cheryl from making direct requests. It brought back all the shame she felt as a teen asking her father for money when he said no—most painfully when she asked him for money to go on a class trip and he said no. It brought back as well the sadness of having to tell her friends that she could not go with them and her loneliness the week they were gone.

I wondered if Cheryl realized that making a request means the other person has the power to say no as well as yes. I asked her if she was making a request or if she were *demanding* that he do something. "I hoped he would agree, but realized he could say no." She took a deep breath and sighed. I asked what the sigh was about. "Maybe I never feel that *I* can say no," Cheryl admitted, "so I resent it from others." Now, another layer surfaced. Cheryl did not allow herself to say no, so she did not think others had the right to either. Furthermore, she felt someone saying no to her request was a sign of disrespect. Working through the body is interesting to me because at each step, the body reveals more of what is being held back.

The next step for Cheryl was to learn to accept a "no" without relapsing into her internal drama of disrespect and powerless. As in learning to make direct requests, gaining the ability to accept a rejected request took three sessions before Cheryl could maintain her poise without crumbling into Mouse. One key to change for Cheryl was to recognize that when her shoulders curled and her chest tightened, she could practice dropping her breath into her belly and get centered. From here she recognized that she felt less afraid. It brought back the memory of how she anchored herself before a track meet in college—the crouch in the blocks before the starting gun. Accessing her center deactivated her Mouse-body, where her breath was high and her chest felt tight. As in making requests, Cheryl found being centered made all the difference in calibrating how forceful to be. Later that day she asked her boss for an additional person. Although he said no, she said the rejection was not hard to take at all. She felt proud of herself for having the courage to make the request.

A few weeks later, I got a surprise telephone call from Cheryl. "This amazing thing happened," she said. "Tom said no to me again."

"Then why do you sound so happy?" I asked.

She related that while making the request she had been able to drop her breath, stand tall, and stay centered the whole time. She felt the strength of her stance made him pay attention to her. Even though he said no, he looked up at her and said courteously, "Sorry, I can't help you this week."

"He was so polite I thought maybe an alien had invaded his body,"

Cheryl joked.

I asked how she felt. She said she felt courageous and inspired to ask for what she wanted and to say no when she needed to. "What does that feel like in your body?" I asked. "I feel tall and powerful like when I crossed the finish line in a race," she said, "like I can take care of myself." Being more effective at leadership and influence made the work juicy for Cheryl.

To achieve our goals or to be who we long to be, we must be able to take new actions. New ways of engaging can feel uncomfortable, sometimes even unsafe. We adopted the old behaviors because at the time they worked and got us what we wanted. Now that they are not working, we still revert to the ineffective behavior because it feels comfortable and the new behavior, while more effective, does not feel right. It may feel like putting on a new pair of shoes that look stylish but do not feel nearly as comfortable as the old shoes we have broken-in. Being centered allows us to try new moves and to make the moves in ways that work. Having a coach as an ally to weather the discomfort of learning new actions and to calibrate how far to go makes it easier to take risks. Consider the pain Cheryl felt at being taken advantage of and feeling unsupported by her peers. To learn that she could get support by behaving differently was a life-changing experience for her. Imagine how many possibilities opened when she became able to make direct requests and decline requests from others.

When we consider that we all have behaviors that limit our effectiveness, we gain an even greater appreciation of the power of somatics to increase our awareness and capacity to change.

Thinking about a change is a necessary step in the process, not an end. Change must be "embodied" if we are to achieve our juicy work. Over time, with practice, new behavior becomes deeply rooted and can be relied on to produce the results we want.

Exercises for diagnosing the knowing-doing gap:

1. Make a list of situations that are not working out in the way you want. Notice if there are common themes to those situations, e.g., direct reports not meeting deadlines that you have assigned, or kids not doing their chores without nagging.
2. Notice when co-workers are more successful with tasks that are difficult for you. Notice how their approach differs from your own.

Exercises for closing the knowing-doing gap:

1. Identify low-risk situations where you can practice new behaviors.
2. Have a trusted friend or co-worker observe you and give you feedback on changes you have identified.

Part 3

Finding and Creating an Ideal Environment

-chapter 6-

From Drama and Trauma to Building Relationships at Work

"Oh, you hate your job? Why didn't you say so? There's a support group for that. It's called everybody, and they meet at the bar."

Drew Carey

Juicy work rarely thrives in an atmosphere characterized by drama and trauma; we do our best work in respectful and collaborative workplaces. For far too many people, drama—giving full range to one's emotions without considering the impact on others—is standard office procedure. While expressing emotions is healthy, living in a constant state of high drama can have harmful effects on your body and on your relationships with others. I think of drama as an addiction to high-intensity negative emotions. Many times politicians use drama to persuasively make a point. During an election, the candidates will say things in a dramatic way that may be misunderstood, like a vote for this candidate will bring about "death panels" for the elderly.

Trauma refers to life experiences that we may or may not have fully resolved. They may even be events we have little awareness of that get reactivated under similar situations. Being unaware of these unresolved traumas often means that we are not fully present in a given situation. We are responding to the past, rather than to the situation as it is and with the intensity it deserves. For example, if growing up you had a very critical parent, a boss giving you feedback may cause you to be much more upset than the situation warrants.

Very often drama can emerge from trauma, leading to sweeping generalizations like "everyone's out to get me," or "no one ever appreciates me," or "everyone else gets promoted except me." Patterns get set up in our youth and we can live out those patterns in an emotional way throughout our adult lives. Drama is often an expression of the trauma of not feeling loved, appreciated, or understood.

When I am coaching someone who seems to be caught up in drama or trauma, what I want to do is help him see how the drama benefits him. If Joe realizes what he is getting from his dramatic behavior, perhaps he can identify another way to achieve the same end without the volatility. If Joe's coworkers understand what he is seeking, perhaps they can provide it before the emotions escalate. In my experience, the drama costs far more than it benefits. Drama- and trauma-free workplaces are efficient and fun—in other words, juicy!

Here are some examples of what drama and trauma look like in the workplace. I coached Gina, who, as a little girl, got praised for making good grades and shamed when she did not. Her parents used sibling rivalry to encourage good performance, and praise for one was always accompanied by disappointment in the others. The child who jumped to meet the parents' request was showered with praise, while those who did not respond as quickly were criticized. Gina showed up at work overachieving, overdoing, never saying no, and needing to be adored by the boss, even though she was putting her health and family at risk and annoying her colleagues, who felt their own contributions were being marginalized by her need to always be in the spotlight.

We worked to uncover the source of her unquenchable thirst for approval, to connect it to her professional life, and to identify the impacts it was having on her colleagues and family.

When we discussed what approval meant to Gina, she could not immediately identify why it mattered. I asked her to recall her first memories of praise and how it felt. As the oldest child, five years older than her closest sibling, she remembered a steady stream of praise and affection from her parents until her brother was born. When another sister came along thirteen months later, she felt completely ignored. She got attention by taking care of her siblings, yet felt ignored and displaced. As her siblings got older she felt she was in competition for the meager scraps of her parent's love. She recognized that she was seeking approval at work from supervisors and that acknowledgement of other employees made her feel undervalued and reminded her of the wound from her family history.

I taught her techniques to become her own source of approval and to build her confidence. She learned to center herself and found that meditation had a positive impact on her. Yet, still, she was drawn to over-commit and to take on too much responsibility, partly to be acknowledged, but also from fear of being criticized or rejected. She found that she was comparing herself to colleagues and resenting all the extra work she was doing. Even though she had a better self im-age, she was still caught up in patterns of taking on too much. I asked her to define a "reasonable" workload. Then I asked what more she was willing to do and to identify why she should do it. As she listed the additional projects and tasks, Gina saw that she was doing some to learn, some because she had the best skill set for the job, and yes, some to get praise. I asked her if she could say no to the last group of activities. She said that when she looked at the underlying reason to do those tasks, she was able to decide on which ones to pass.

Gina was able to put her drama in its place and to develop bound-aries, to let colleagues shine too, and to pay attention to her own needs and the needs of her family. She realized she could say no to others without needing their approval, and she grew to understand and ac-cept why others might say no to her requests. No one was trying to sabotage her, she realized, and ultimately her whole work team was able to operate more effectively and in greater total balance. Once it is clear what the issue is that is causing the drama, we can use exercises and awareness to build a more effective way of dealing with situations. We do not have to resort to drama to get our needs met.

A manager I worked with had a father who never gave him praise.

When I started working with this manager, he criticized his employees until they felt like they could not succeed, that nothing they did was good enough. He had no idea how dismissive he was. I sat with Betsy, one of his employees, during a 360 degree feedback review where she received mostly high marks from others but very low marks from him. "I think it's time to update my resume," she said glumly when we went over the scores.

Every time I had talked with her boss, however, he told me what a good job she was doing. We discussed what his scores could mean, and after we reviewed the actual work she had completed to his satisfaction, I managed to help her put her boss's scores in perspective. Then I put a call in to her boss. "I talked Betsy off the ledge," I told him, "but she's coming to meet with you tomorrow to discuss her work performance. You need to let her know how you really feel about her."

He was unconcerned. "She's new, she can't be doing all that well," he explained, adding "She understands how I grade."

While he had not intended to hurt his employee's feelings, that is exactly what he did. A little piece of Betsy's heart got crushed that day and he paid it no mind. At the end of our conversation about the purpose of 360 degree reviews I asked him whether he wanted to change his rating to be more consistent with the other scores. I knew he was on a short list of promotion candidates so I added, "Judging employees too harshly where they feel unable to succeed and having resultant high turnover can significantly derail your promotion."

He replied, "If I have to change who I am to get promoted, something's wrong."

Something was wrong all right. His attitude revealed unresolved trauma stemming from how he was raised—he got along fine without being praised by his father, so why should he be expected to praise anyone else? Now, that trauma had become part of his management style. He was an exceptional consultant who brought in a lot of business, but as a manager he was a jerk. His insensitivity was bravado and when he was not promoted he was crushed. His boss told him he was passed over because he did not motivate and develop staff. This time he took in the impact of his harshness with staff and was willing to work on it. We began to work on his management style and he did not resist. Eventually he did get promoted and he realized that he had been his own worst enemy.

The biggest challenge with drama and trauma behaviors is helping people recognize them. Often, when I point out this type of drama, a client's reaction is denial, defensiveness, or contempt for others. What I help them do is to stay open and centered so that these behaviors do not close off possibilities for their future, or take them off their path. It is important to recognize the behaviors but not be pulled down by them. If people understand how what they are doing is getting in the way, they can change their behavior, have a healthier relationship with their coworkers, and work more effectively at the task at hand.

Another way drama and trauma show up is when a manager consciously or unconsciously causes conflict between employees. For example, a manager may unwittingly assign the same work to two people, setting up a competition between employees and potentially destroying their working relationship. Again, this behavior may be rooted in a family issue: perhaps a parent compared siblings to each other rather than accepting each individual as unique. Tom was never praised for being a great ball player without Larry being criticized for being so clumsy. Likewise, Larry was never praised for his good grades without Tom being told he was not measuring up in intelligence. When a manager gives the same job to two people, he also could be reenacting his childhood fears of failure and trying to make doubly sure that the work will get done.

Part of our growth process is working on those areas that are underdeveloped and starting to heal old traumas so we can pursue a more productive work and personal life. Finding out what triggers the drama or the trauma in ourselves is a beginning step to help us fundamentally change our old way of being to one that is more constructive.

As a coach, I concentrate on the behavior and avoid putting a name on it. I do not say, "My goodness, you really are insecure," when a manager frets that his team will not complete an important task. Instead I say, "Tell me about your experiences. What experiences do you have that make you believe subordinates won't follow through on tasks?" In many cases, it will come down to one single, isolated unresolved life event that is the source of his concern. Through questioning he invariably realizes there are many more times when his team succeeded than when they let him down.

"Notice how you're holding on to this version of events," I tell him. "In spite of irrefutable data that people do come through, there's a part of you that still believes that's not the case. What would it take for you to hold yourself more open to believing that people will come through for you?" We tried some experiments. For example, I had the manager give assignments to one employee at a time and build in safety nets to make sure he gets the deliverable he needs. The safety net might simply be a regular status meeting with the employee. Or it might mean a delivery date two to three days before the actual deadline so the manager has time to fix anything that is not quite right. I helped him design processes to ensure that he will get what he wants.

Sometimes managers have very black-and-white thinking: the employee will do it or the employee will not. I can trust this person and not that one. That mindset does not consider the circumstances that generate one person's success and another person's failure. The question is not who will succeed and who will fail, but rather, "How can I set up a process that ensures everyone's success?"

One technique is to go a couple of layers beneath "I trust this person" or "I don't trust this person" and ask, "What leads me to trust one person and not the other? What evidence do I have that one person is trustworthy and the other is not? What could I do differently with the person I don't trust to get a better response?" For example, I may determine that Jane is trustworthy because she is a creative thinker. When a roadblock occurs, Jane is able to find two or three different ways to get something done. I do not trust Jennifer because she does not have that level of creativity. What I could do to increase Jennifer's trust ability is to encourage her to do more creative problem solving so that when she hits a wall, she does not stop. I think she will find alternative solutions if she stays with the problem longer. I could also look for creativity training for her.

One client said to me: "We have to hire A+ employees in this organization, because only A+ employees can navigate all the hurdles." That is placing a lot of pressure on the employees. Any employee can succeed if the company removes the right hurdles. People feel powerless in environments without strong processes and systems, so they keep doing what they have always done, like micromanaging or giving the same assignment to multiple people. They are not bad people, but they do not see another way to operate.

A manager told me a story about two employees who were not speaking to each other. One was a project manager on the team, and the other was a more senior program manager. The project manager's task was to write down the action items that resulted from team meetings. She was not well versed in the technical aspects at the program level, and when she sent out the minutes of their meetings the program manager sent replies to the whole team correcting her mistakes. Embarrassed, the project manager asked if the program manager would review her minutes before she sent them out. The program manager would not hear of it and said the project manager was being overly sensitive. They were at a stalemate.

The program manager's unwillingness to help a colleague or even appreciate her embarrassment could stem from many sources. It is not always necessary to know the reason behind a given trauma or drama. Rather than getting stuck in analysis, create a workaround. When people keep doing their drama and trauma behaviors over and over they remind me of those windup toys that go as fast as they can, hit a wall, go as fast as they can, hit another wall and then flip over, wheels spinning until they are out of energy. If they were going in a different direction instead of ramming themselves headlong against the same two walls, they might be able to get somewhere.

When faced with the kind of black–and–white thinking that had brought the program manager and the project manager to their stalemate, I ask, "What's a third option?" Often I find it useful to illustrate the issue with approximation points. I draw a line with option A at one end and option B at the other. For example, if option A is not loaning money to your brother-in-law, and option B is giving your brother-in-law all the money he is asking for, what are some other options along the way? This exercise requires that people emotionally unhook themselves and become objective enough to pull themselves out of their black-and-white thinking.

In the situation between the project and program managers, the project manager said, "I'm being humiliated by being corrected in front of the whole team." The program manager is essentially saying, "This is what works for me and I'm not willing to change my approach." Someone outside of their impasse can come up with a dozen approximation points as alternate options. The project manager could go to another team member who understands the substantive points, rather than going to the program manager. Or, the notes could go out under the program manager's name instead of the project manager's name. You and I could spend an hour coming up with options because we are unencumbered by the emotional aspects of this relationship.

Professional coaches are not emotionally encumbered by their clients' situations. Among coaches there is considerable controversy about whether people should talk about their feelings. Some will say, "That's therapy! I don't want therapy! I want coaching." Feelings have a huge impact in the business realm, however, and I believe a good coach—and healthy employees—cannot ignore them.

As managers and colleagues, we need to speak with people about emotions in a way that is not perceived as simply touchy-feely. During the conversation, stay with the data and acknowledge how the person feels. "I can see why you would feel hurt," I might tell a client who felt slighted by a colleague. Then I add, "Now, let's examine what about the action hurt you, and what you want to do about it." When we have constructive ways to bring feelings to feedback conversations, we can begin to redirect drama and trauma behavior and create lasting change.

Recognizing Stress and Trauma

I find that many people use work or "busyness" as an excuse for not feeling something. As long as they are really busy, they do not stop to realize, "I hate my job," or "I'm not good at what I am doing," or "I don't like the people I work with." They are hiding any number of negative feelings that they hold inside and do not express. While they are not expressing their misgivings directly, it is undoubtedly showing up physically. People may be overweight, suffer heart attacks, have high blood pressure—there is a huge list of ailments and physical challenges that can come from suppressing emotions. While the solution to the problem may require some behavior change that you are afraid of or are uncomfortable with, it is the kind of change you will look back on later and thank your body for sending you the warning signals.

Leslie suffered from neck and back pain that was only getting worse and worse. She had to turn her whole body just to talk to someone face to face. She was in pain 24 hours a day. Her doctors told her the only way she might get relief is to have her vertebrae fused. Leslie realized how much she hated her job and how much she missed her kids during the six weeks she spent recuperating from the operation. She got well and quit. It was the best thing she ever did. The "do it, do it now, do it faster" pace at the job never gave her the time to stop and think about what was really happening. It took a serious operation to get her to stop and think about what her body was telling her.

Jack was a senior vice president in an organization that was going through lay-offs. He was concerned about losing his job even though he was a top performer and led the company's biggest product line. As a result, he was taking credit for the work of his staff and not acknowledging them. In meetings with peers he interrupted to make his point to be sure that the Chief Operating Officer knew how smart he was. When we began the coaching engagement, he started by telling me how bad things were and how concerned he was for his job and the company. I was getting depressed just listening to him speak. I knew I had to shift his mood (and mine) to make progress.

I asked him to describe the best job he ever had. I wanted to know about the work he was doing then, how he was doing it, what colleagues were like, his boss, his clients and his direct reports. He told an engaging story of a high-trust, highly collaborative work environment. As he spoke, his shoulders relaxed, his eyes softened, and his demeanor went from stiff and cold to warm and passionate. What a change! I asked him how much of the things he liked were evident in his current job. He admitted that few of the factors that made the other job exceptional were present. I asked him how much influence he had in the quality of his work life and after some reflection he started identifying things he could do to improve his situation.

He brought his team together and admitted his fears about the lay-offs. They were concerned, too. He identified two things that were hurting the company-poor quality products leading to returns and too broad a product line with little differentiation between products. With lay-offs there were not enough people for all of the work, so quality suffered. His team attacked the product line issue first and reduced the number of products by thirty percent, keeping the most popular products and those with the highest margin. They could concentrate on quality and get it right now with fewer products. Jack and his team saw a way to succeed, help the company, and keep their jobs by focusing on what he could control and having a vision for improvement. Too often people get caught by fear and can only fight, flee or freeze. When Jack remembered how resourceful and effective he had been in the past, he was able to see what was possible. His competitive behavior fell away as positive motivation replaced the fear. He turned his company around and no other jobs were lost.

Sophia had been a senior consultant for eight years. She was moved to a new team and a new market that she knew nothing about. Initially she was excited about learning something new, and then she got a new boss, Larry. Larry had years of experience in that particular market and she thought he would have contacts that, with her deep expertise, could be very useful towards her success. Larry would meet with clients and come back and ask her to write a white paper on how they could help. He gave Sophia only the most meager information and she did her best, but she did not understand the issues well enough based on Larry's reports from the meetings. He did not understand her functional expertise well enough to leverage it. Her requests for Larry to take her to the meetings were denied. Larry became more critical of Sophia's work and she could not find a way to improve. All of her suggestions were ignored. At her next meeting with Larry, he told her he was putting her on a performance plan and she had ninety days to bring in business or lose her job. Sophia was in tears when she told me the news.

I asked her what she wanted. She said she wanted to be successful again and she felt she could not be under Larry's management. She could not go to another internal team in the company now that she was on a performance plan. She felt like her only option was to leave before she got fired.

Sophia was the main breadwinner for her family. They counted on her income to survive. I asked her what she knew she was good at doing. She gave me four examples of client situations where she had done exceptional work. "What about winning business?" I asked. She acknowledged that she did not like selling and did not feel good at it. We brainstormed options – she could take a demotion where selling was not expected, she could learn to sell, or she could look for another job. Sophia felt undervalued in the company that she had done so much for in the past and she felt she had no option but to leave. I encouraged her to learn to sell while she was job hunting and she readily agreed.

She could not get work from Larry's contacts, which he refused to provide, but she had a strong network of people in the company and in client organizations. We discussed ways she could connect with them and what she would say. She thought that to sell you had to go in and convince people that they should buy what you are offering. I offered her an alternative view, that selling was listening to clients' needs and making offers when something they needed was what you could offer. I showed her how that would also work in interviewing—not selling yourself, but rather, listening to what the organization needed and providing examples of how you could help. Sophia could see a way forward that was consistent with her skills and values. In two months time she had two job offers and had sold the amount of work required to keep her current job. She was happy that she sold the work because she did not want a negative mark on her prior stellar career performance. She had lost faith, however, in the organization that had put her in an untenable position with a poor manager. After carefully reviewing her job options, she went with a company that wanted her for her functional expertise. She interviewed with several senior people there and asked about their philosophy toward developing employees. She made sure that they were as interested in fostering their staff as they were in making money. She feels appreciated in her new job and is once again doing juicy work.

Drama and trauma at work, while uncomfortable, are often a gateway to real learning and interpersonal growth. Learning to confront and defuse drama and trauma is a skill that is invaluable in any organization. Learning to confront it in yourself is one of the greatest skills of self-awareness you can cultivate. When you see how you are being affected by the workplace, you can consider if you can create a healthy 'micro-climate' where you and others will thrive or if another organization would suit you better.

A Novel Solution

I have found that drama and trauma are reduced by love. Yes, love. What I mean is to see the goodness in people, even when they are not showing their best self. I look for the seed of caring that wants to be expressed and I encourage people to show that part of themselves. I look for the best in people and stay away from being critical or judgmental. I have a belief that people are doing the best they can at any given moment, and that if they could do better, they would. When people feel cared about, they show up differently than when they feel criticized. Creating a mood of acceptance and appreciation lessens the drama and trauma.

Exercises for reducing drama and trauma:

1. Focus on the positive - research shows that a positive mindset leads to more creative thinking and helps others find solutions. Every day ask, "What is one thing I can do to create a more positive environment?" Then implement your ideas.

2. Let people know the impact of their behavior on you in a constructive way. If someone yells at me, I say, "I want to hear what you have to say, but I can't hear it at that volume." If someone complains about another employee, I do not get drawn into the criticism. I ask, "What could we do to help that person?" Reframing the conversational tone to one that conveys support changes the dynamic.

3. Notice your mood. Each day make a note of how you are feeling. The greater access you have to your feelings, the better you will be able to recognize how you may be affecting others.

4. Do a GAP analysis each day. The GAP analysis reminds you of what is working and builds self-esteem. Try this daily reflection:
   G - Today, I am **G**rateful for…
   A - Today, I **A**ccomplished…
   P - Today, I am **P**roud that…

5. Create a positive climate. Notice and appreciate what is working. Thank people for their work. Make sure you say three positive comments for each constructive one. Research shows that it takes three positives to equal one constructive for the person receiving the feedback.

-chapter 7-

The Learning Mindset

*"In the beginner's mind there are many possibilities.
In the expert's mind, there are few."*
Chinese proverb

When people approach a new learning opportunity confident in what they already know (without feeling the need to point it out), curious to find out what they do not know, and excited to learn from others, they have what I call the "learning mindset." They are eager to discuss what they know and do not know with other people on the learning path. They realize learning is not about competition or looking down on other people while proudly standing on what they know; rather, it is about being open to learning so they can travel to a space of even deeper and richer knowledge than they currently occupy.

When a learning mindset prevails, the masters, the teachers, and the students are indistinguishable in their openness to learning. I have gone to some workshops where the mindset of the instructor is: "You are empty pitchers. Sit and absorb what I have to offer." The teacher's need for the student to be empty, to have no prior knowledge, deliberately ignores the path that brought the student to that learning opportunity, and it sets up a negative dynamic. Even if the participants have a learning mindset, an instructor without that openness invariably shuts down any possibilities outside of her own understanding. Her response to a participant's alternative ideas reveals a closed mindset. "Well, I've been doing this for thirty years," she might say, or "I've worked with Fortune 50 companies on this process." There is a resistance to thinking there might be something she does not know. If the instructor has nothing to work on, if they already know it all, there is no opening for learning, there is no place to go. When the instructor does not model openness to learning, it makes it harder for the students to learn. The student's natural curiosity can be stifled by an instructor who is unwilling to consider that there may be alternate possibilities to the one he or she presented.

What do you need to get yourself there?

The learning mindset is about keeping curiosity alive. What does it take? Why do some people continue to go deeper in learning and head for mastery, where others merely dabble? In George Leonard's book *Mastery*, he talks about the different learning styles. Some people stay on the surface of things, some people jump from thing to thing and they never learn deeply enough to become a master at anything. Juicy work requires a balance between learning and implementing. Too little learning makes the work product stale. Too much learning and you may not get anything out the door.

A book called *Mindset* by Carol Dweck compares learners and performers. The author defines performers as being focused on how to look good and stay in their comfort zone. She calls this a fixed mindset. They seek to do what they already know as well as they possibly can. Performers are great when they are in their zone, but if the job changes and they have to change what they do and how they do it, problems arise. (Peter Drucker, a leadership theorist, coined this "the Peter Principal," where people rise to their level of incompetence.) She defines learners as having a growth mindset. Learners, unlike performers, are more interested in the process than the in the outcome.

Making a mistake or failing is part of the learning process and has no negative stigma. The problem is that a growth mindset, if taken to extreme, may make people so interested in learning that they do not pay attention to outcomes. They are interested, they are curious, but they are not goal oriented.

In the information technology world, these are the folks who spend days and days learning new technology but they never get around to sitting down and writing computer programs. We can be learners in one area of our life and performers in others, or access both mindsets, depending on the goal. When I am cooking dinner during the week, I am performing - making the dinners I know I can make quickly that will satisfy my family. When I cook on weekends, the learner comes out and I try new recipes and play with ingredients just for the fun of it.

Each person's penchant for learning differentiates his or her experience. A friend of mine, Jake, created a handheld device. He was interested in brain research and wanted to apply that learning to technology so people could have information in their palms. He achieved his goal, but he did not stay to develop the next-generation devices. He wrote a book and started an institute on brain research. Another friend, Bruce, is an entrepreneur. He has started ten to twelve companies; some have been wildly successful and others have failed. What Bruce is good at is recognizing what it takes for the companies to succeed and knowing when he cannot save the company and moving on. The key to Jake and Bruce's success is that they each recognize their strengths, passions, and environment and when those conditions are not met they move on. Both of them are learners - taking what they know, stretching it and applying it in new and interesting ways.

Another colleague is clearly a performer. She is an expert in networking and has taken this skill in many directions - teaching, keynote performances, books on the topic and using the skill to build her business. She stays in a narrow niche where she is exceedingly competent and does not build additional skills or go away from her performance area.

To avoid the performer/learner hazard, ask yourself: "Am I going too far in one direction or the other? What do I need to achieve better balance?" For a learner who likes to dabble in many things, a coach might help her find a career that better values that approach, such as a Montessori teacher who helps children explore in the moment. Or, depending on their skillset, learners might flourish working for a think tank. Their whole job might be to come up with creative ideas while someone else focuses on implementation and product development. The point is that you don't necessarily have to change your mindset, instead, find a place where your mindset is valued. If you are a learner and you are building tract homes, you are probably not feeling very fulfilled with your work. With each house, you want to do things a little differently, but being a successful tract homes builder means creating a consistent, replicable product that works over and over again—an approach that is perfect for a performer, not a learner.

If you lean heavily towards being a performer, are you no longer able to perform because the field has changed and you do not "get it" anymore? If so, you have a couple of options. Perhaps you could bring your skill to an organization that is not so sophisticated. Advanced technology has changed the way many sophisticated organizations are doing business. If you go to a startup, small association, or mid-sized company, what you know may be exactly what they need for their business. Instead of moving up to more sophisticated organizations when you hit the wall of your knowledge, move down to less sophisticated organizations where your skills and expertise are still valued.

If you feel like you are too experienced to learn new things, I would focus on what excites you. If learning creates a fear, such as the fear of looking foolish, find a safe place in which to practice. Some organizations have long memories for mistakes and shorter memories for successes. There can be a greater risk in trying something new and failing rather than sticking with something that works, so finding a safe way to practice new learning skills is essential.

For example, I worked with a manager who was very good at giving orders and being direct. He was given a new team of very strong performers who tended to be collaborative and facilitative. He did not know how to function in that environment, but he did not want to appear weak or ineffective. I suggested that he find a way to practice teamwork where the level of expectation was lower and less was at stake, career-wise, if he came up short. The perfect opportunity arose when his church was looking for a committee to conduct a fundraising drive. He stepped up to lead the fund drive team, which allowed him to become more familiar with collaboration. Later, he could bring the skills he learned back to his organization, confident in his abilities.

But what if, after practicing with his church committee, this person realized he is terrible at facilitation and that he will never get the hang of it and in fact he hates it. Then, his best option would be to find a company where they really need someone who has a direct approach and go be the best at it. That is called playing to your strengths.

As mentioned, we do not always know what our strengths are, but self-assessment tools are available that can help. The Gallup Organization offers two books—*Now Discover Your Strengths* and *StrengthsFinder 2.0*, that define 34 different strengths. The assessments identify your top five strengths. One of my top five is positivity, always seeing the glass half full, which explains why I look for a client's strengths and help them understand how to apply them. When people know their strengths, it helps them find joy at work.

If knowing your strengths is helpful, what about knowing your weaknesses, or as one woman put it: "What are my five worst strengths?" She figured that if she could improve her weaknesses she might find more satisfaction in her work. The goal of the Strengths Finder instrument is not to identify weak areas, it is to understand how your strengths can best be applied. What does it help me to know that my five worst sporting events are football, basketball, soccer, track, and shot-put when I have no interest or desire to play these sports?

Of course it can be helpful to be aware of your weaker areas. If I am launching a new business and I know I am not good at finance, it means I need to hire people who have expertise in that area. As a coach, I believe it is essential to focus not on weaknesses, which lead clients to feel bad about themselves, but rather to highlight strengths, because people often resist accepting and celebrating them. Acknowledging and building on strengths is fundamental to a learning mindset.

A client told me a story about working with a programmer who was brilliant but who rubbed everyone the wrong way. They were paired to deliver a new version of software that would improve time reporting. The clients were nervous about the software and concerned that it would not meet all of their needs and would be difficult to implement. She told the programmer, "We've got to work together to make this work. My ability to work well with people combined with your technology skills is a winning combination." She did not take his gruffness personally and stayed focused on the goal. She made sure that he realized they were working toward the same goal by asking him how she could help him and by delivering on his requests. He asked her to keep the clients happy and off his back. He appreciated her client handling skills and she got to the goodness underneath his crusty exterior.

Later, when she had a boss she was not working with effectively, I asked her, "What if your boss were like this programmer, what would you do?" She was surprised, because she had been willing to adjust her work style with her peers and direct reports, and she expected her boss would adjust his style to match hers as well. She had been waiting for her boss to figure this out and the more she sat and waited, the more frustrated she got. Finally she realized her boss did not have the same ability she had to recognize and adjust to someone else's work style. She would have to take a direct approach. When she asked for what she needed, her boss was happy to give it to her.

We may assume bosses know more than we do and that they are supposed to help us. When my client realized that help can go both up and come down the organization structure, new possibilities opened up to her. This happened with another client who was frustrated: he and his team were trying to move forward but were waiting on a strategy from the Executive VP above him. I asked him, "Aren't you good at strategy?" He said, "Yeah, I'm great at it." "So why are you waiting for this guy?" I replied. He wrote the strategy and worked it with the team. When he showed it to his boss, his boss was so excited about it that he showed it to other EVPs. In addition to moving the project forward, my client got substantial credit for his strategic thinking.

Having a learning mindset can mean shifting your point of view, as in the example above, or it can mean seeing new possibilities. Some people are scared about this economy. I asked one of my clients about his business and he said, "This is a great time for us. We're consultants and when people are worried about the future that is when we can offer businesses the most help." When I asked another client whose organization was about to announce layoffs, he told me his position was secure but he was concerned about the impact the layoff would have on other people. I knew he had been laid off earlier in his career, so I asked if that experience had any positive aspects. "It made me realize I can always find another job. I know how to survive. I know that I can make it in the world." He went on to describe five or six benefits, including the opportunity to transition to a new industry that was a better fit for him. I asked him, "Would you have made that transition by choice?" He said, "Probably not." Then I asked, "Looking back, if you had a choice, would you rather have been laid off or not?" He thought a moment and said, "I'd rather have been laid off." I suggested that he share his story with people as they go through the layoff process to help them see that there can be opportunity even in a difficult situation.

You can engage your learning mindset by reflecting on a past change. Think about a change you underwent and ask yourself:

- How am I different now?
- Would I have learned what I learned if I had not gone through the experience?
- What was the worst thing that happened from that experience?
- What was the best thing that happened?

Stay open to the possibilities of what you can learn and gain from your difficult experiences and think about all the things that have served you during difficult times. What were the resources that helped you get through the last difficult challenge you faced, whether it was a difficult boss, an irritating coworker, or an unsupportive work situation? You might say, "I have great friends," or "I have a coach," or "I started networking and talked to people I hadn't seen in a long time. Those people led me to opportunities I might not have seen otherwise." We have amazing resources we can bring to bear but we often forget how helpful they were after the problem is resolved.

We go through a lot of pain in our lives and some of us forget about it once we have experienced it. We forget the struggle. We lose the opportunity to call on those resources when we face another challenge when we forget the struggle and how we got through it. In our memories we make the experience scarier than it was and the solution elusive.

When someone is stuck in fear, I have him consider the worst-case scenario. "So you lose your job, what's the worst thing that will happen?" I ask. "I'd lose my house," one executive responded. "Then what would you do?" I persisted. "We would rent until I get another good job." This analysis helped him face the worst possible outcome and see his way past it. He had a six-figure income, substantial savings, and all he can see is his family on the street. The fear, while real, was getting in the way of his seeing solutions.

I asked a client who had an MBA from Harvard and an engineering degree to make a list of fifteen things she could do if she were not working in her current industry. By the time she reached twenty job possibilities, she realized what a joke it was to imagine herself living on the street if she were to lose her job.

If you listen to the news or read the paper, it sometimes sounds like it is all gloom and doom and the world will soon come to an end. Negative thinking stimulates more negative thinking. If you have a positive mindset, you think about what is possible and do not allow fear-based thinking to affect you.

When my grandparents talked about the Great Depression, they would recall getting together with friends and family to play Scrabble or dominoes. They did not dwell on whether they were deprived. People would come to the door, and they would give them work and feed them.

Even in those difficult times, some positive things emerged: friendships grew stronger and people learned to sew, crochet, can fruits, and grow vegetables. People faced with adversity discovered how resilient they were. They realize that being with family is comforting and that helping people who are worse off than they gives them perspective and solace. Some deprivations can turn out to be beneficial. My grandmother recalled that her family did not have meat at every meal. She lived to be ninety-four years old. Now, decades later, many nutritionists recommend we eat less meat and include more meatless meals in our diet!

Remember how many changes you have gone through in your life. It seems easy when you look back, but it seems so difficult when you are going through them. I remember thinking how hard college was and wondering if I would ever get through it. Or how difficult a bad marriage can be, and how painful it is when it ends in divorce, or how stressful it can be to care for an elderly parent or a sick child. The average person goes through hundreds of these transitions in a lifetime, but the one you are in at the time is the one that seems to overwhelm you. Maybe it is because the ones you have come through have shaped you in some way. You are more self-reliant, more flexible, and more humble. You have strengths you did not have before but you forgot where you learned the lesson.

If you replay that difficult situation, and what you did to get yourself through it, it builds confidence. There is a technique in neuro-linguistic programming (NLP) called creating a "resource state." You vividly recall a time when you were successful and immerse yourself in the memory utilizing all your senses—how you felt about yourself, what the world looked like and felt like to you then, what your internal dialogue was, and what others were saying to you. Practice doing this over and over so you can recreate the physiology of that experience. Then you apply that same mindset to a new situation so you can bring that same level of confidence and strength.

I applied the resource state with a client who had to make a presentation to three hundred people and was shaking in his boots. I asked him, "What's the biggest group you ever spoke to?" "Fifty people at the Rotary," he replied. "How did it go?" I asked. "Great," he said, so I asked him to tell me about another time he made a presentation. "Well, I talked to a group about data security and they loved it." After just a few minutes he had several examples of his own success in presentations. Then I asked what made those presentations go well, what did he do, how did he achieve success? I asked him to describe those presentations in detail; what he saw in the room, what he heard, what he was saying to himself, how he felt. I took notes of each situation and probed for as much detail as he could remember. Then I asked him to come up with a physical touch that could remind him of the experience, or anchor it. Some people touch their watch or ring or connect finger to thumb. The touch needs to be subtle and easy to do in any situation. We are not looking for obvious signals like catchers give to the pitcher to tell them what kind of ball to throw.

After getting details on his successful presentations, I asked him to close his eyes as I read the successes back to him. When the first successful presentation was recalled, I had him take a deep breath and touch his anchor. Then I read the second one, and again, had him take a deep breath and touch his anchor. The third scenario was recalled, with the anchor. Then I described the situation that was coming up with three hundred people and used words from his prior successes to link to the new situation. Again, I asked him to take a deep breath and to touch his anchor. After opening his eyes, he said he felt centered and confident that he could do the presentation. I asked him to review the successes each day at least twice while taking a deep breath and touching his anchor until the day of the presentation and that when he walked to the podium to immediately take a deep breath and touch his anchor.

He realized his fear was unfounded, but he knew he would always be a little nervous when making presentations. "That's okay," I said, many actors admit that they are often a little scared when they first step onto a stage. In fact, they say that when the day comes that they are not nervous, they should quit because being in front of an audience no longer gets their heart pumping. When he presented to the large group, he remembered how it felt to succeed (not fears or failure) and he did well. He was still nervous, but relaxed as he spoke. He is eager to present again.

I was working with a young man who was preparing to talk to a prospective client about coaching with the expectation that if his presentation went well he might get some business. He was a student in the Georgetown University coaching program at the time. I asked him to imagine a time he felt really comfortable talking to prospective clients. He talked about doing brown bag lunchtime talks on different aspects of leadership and how much he enjoyed conducting them. The companies he did brown bags for gave him access to potential clients in exchange for him sharing his expertise in an area that interested them. This became his resource state. He prepared for his presentation by remembering the positive brown bag experiences and feeling how successful he was in that realm. When he did the coaching presentation for the prospective client, the clients were so impressed that they asked him to do coaching in their organization. He went from being afraid he would blow the presentation to winning a client.

We are always practicing something, rehearsing in our mind. What we typically rehearse are the times we screwed up. The resource state allows us to rehearse something that went well. After all, what will help you do your best, thinking about limitations and failures or thinking about how you were successful?

We all have expectations in life. We might expect to meet interesting new people or just have a good time when we go to a party. Or we might expect to be alone and uncomfortable and have a miserable time. Chances are, if we go in expecting to have a miserable time, we will probably behave in a way that brings that situation about. As a coach, my goal is to help people imagine good outcomes, to prepare for the best instead of the worst.

The bottom line is that preparation is a part of learning. Our mindset creates our reality. The way we think has a huge impact on the way we behave and the way things turn out for us. Whatever we think we can do, we can, and whatever we think we cannot do, we absolutely cannot.

Historical memories create an initial mindset. By showing people they have choices to do things differently, they find that they can. The learning mindset gives people options where they did not see any. If the only vegetables you have ever had came from a can, and someone offers you fresh vegetables, it is a brand new experience. Once you offer people possibilities, it is up to them to choose what to do with them. The ways things are currently done are not necessarily the way they always have to be done. It is always worth trying something to see if it works. That is the essence of the learning mindset. It is how you can realize possibilities that are better than anything you could ever imagine and far more satisfying than anything you have ever experienced before.

Exercises for stretching your mindset:

Performers (Fixed Mindset)
1. Clarify your goals 3-5 years out. Identify the skills and experiences you will need to get there. Stretch yourself early.
2. Notice what stops you from taking risks and/or learning. Is it fear, lack of learning strategies, impatience? Find people who are not challenged in that area and ask them to share their strategies with you.

Learners (Growth mindset)
1. Ask yourself if you are leveraging your learning or merely learning for learning's sake? What might you be able to accomplish by using the skills you have learned before learning new ones?
2. How is your career enhanced or limited by your mindset. If it is limited, what action could you take to improve?

-epilogue-

Juicy Work in Any Economy

Right now, with the economy causing turmoil in all sectors, you might wonder if searching for your juicy work is the right thing to do. You may think you should just hunker down and hold on to whatever job you have, even if it makes you unhappy. If you have lost a job you have always hated, you may not want to admit that, along with feeling scared and worried, you are a tiny bit relieved.

My guidance is to take this opportunity to clarify what it is you want. If you are employed, take a hard look at what you are doing and ask, "Is this really what I want?" If the honest answer is no, start thinking creatively about what changes you can make at work to make things better, or prepare to look for a better job.

If you have been laid off and are currently in your job search, this is a wonderful time to get creative and analyze the path on which you have been traveling. How did you end up in this situation? Were you in the wrong company and did not see the handwriting on the wall earlier? Or did you not distinguish yourself as much as you could have? Would now be the time to finally consider that alternate path you have daydreamed about? Some people get severance packages. Use the time and money wisely. Work with a coach, explore new possibilities, try an internship or apprentice to someone doing what you think you would like to do.

If you are thinking, "I just need to hurry up and get a job," make sure your haste does not land you in the same, or worse, circumstances. Take time to learn and explore so that you can find a job that is a better fit. Do not exchange one bad thing with another; make an improvement. What can you do that would be more than just fixing your situation, that would improve your situation or at least put you on a path to get where you have really wanted to be all along? You can replace the job that went away, or you can retool with a chance to gain a higher level of juiciness in your work.

In his book *Transitions*, William Bridges talks about people who are so anxious about transitions that they rush from the ending of an unsuccessful situation into a new beginning and find themselves in the same circumstances that created the previous breakdown. If you can tolerate a transition long enough to analyze what brought you to it, you can better understand how to avoid repeating the scenario in your next undertaking.

Telling the truth in the analysis often takes a third party viewpoint. Therapists and coaches are helpful to keep you from repeating the same mistakes and understanding the underlying causes that may have lead you in the wrong direction. You might review the Learning Mindset chapter. Curiosity is a great way to break through patterns of behavior to create something new.

There are numerous things we learn in our body that we do not learn in our heads. It is not just learning things with our mind, but letting a new modality teach us. As the people in Chapter 4 found, the body can be a great teacher if we know how to understand what it is trying to tell us.

Another thing that supports finding juicy work is having enough time to pause and reflect. When people work long hours, they do not have time to stop and think. Sometimes people will get sick or injured, and they will have a long recovery. All of a sudden, insights and ideas start popping out, perhaps because they were too busy before to even think about making a change.

For some people, losing a job makes them realize they really did like their job. Why not take stock of what you have now, appreciate it and be grateful for it? Sometimes we focus on change, but different is not necessarily better.

The economy affects businesses just as it affects careers. Look around and you will see marginal stores going out of business and restaurants that were not at the top of their game shuttered. Why are some companies succeeding while others are not? Recently, I asked a partner at a consulting firm if he was worried about the economy. He said no, adding that a troubled economy is good for his firm because that is when businesses are ready to make changes in order to survive and grow. "When companies are fearful, that's when we do our best work," he explained, "by helping them reduce costs, improve networking and increase sales."

When I visited another firm, I learned the economy was causing them to layoff many people, and those who had survived were overworked and constantly worried. While it may have been the best of times for one company, it was the worst of times for another, even though both were in the same industry and in the same market. There is opportunity even in bad economies, but you have to be open to them and positioned to take advantage of them. That means both your body and your mind have to be open to the possibilities as well as the risks.

Yet, some people and some organizations thrive regardless of external circumstances. When you are successfully doing work that you love, people come to you with job offers. When your company is thriving, other companies want to buy it. Juicy work and juicy work places come from learning, growing and renewal - always wanting to improve and get to the next level.

If you are wondering whether to make a career change, despite or because of the economy, you should thoroughly examine the positives and negatives to assess the risks. What do you know and what are the uncertainties? What are the potential gains? What are the possible losses? If I had never started my own business, I would always have wondered whether I had missed out on something. To think that I had arrived at the end of my life and regretted not having tried—it just was not something I was willing to do. Another way to look at it is to ask, "What's the risk of not doing something?" Sometimes companies only assess the risk of an action, but not the risk of inaction. If their competitor decided to invest in a new extension of their key product, would they lose market share to their competitor? It might be too risky to allow someone else to beat you in the marketplace where you are a leader.

The key to finding juicy work is to have a vision of where you want to go. Energy follows attention. If you put all your attention on what could go wrong, how scared you are, you create a negative swirl of attention that could bring about what you fear most. If instead you create a positive vision, you have the energy to recognize opportunities and to project confidence to which others will be attracted. When other people catch a whiff of the juiciness you are pursuing, they are likely to want a taste as well. You can do this. It is within your reach. You have the power!

About the Author

Sandy Mobley has spent much of her life on a personal quest for juicy work. With bachelors and masters degrees in mathematics and computer science, she started as a computer programmer and moved into technical marketing. She excelled at the work, not for her technical expertise, but rather, in her ability to motivate people to accept technological change. After seven years in technology and feeling burned out, she went back to school for a masters in business administration from Harvard University.

At Harvard, Sandy learned that good organizations focused on people development and that she had a gift for developing people. Her passion was engaged when she joined Hewlett Packard and led executive development and major organizational change initiatives. She was able to build on her technical skills and leverage her MBA to support technical executives in becoming strong leaders. At Hewlett Packard, she was able to use simulations, experiential exercises, and action learning to address the whole person.

She stretched again by starting up training and education for Watson Wyatt and learned how to sell and implement training in a consulting environment. She designed and delivered over 55 programs in two years and became adept at tailoring the training to the group in the moment. This skill was honed further as she moved to McKinsey & Company as a director of training.

Her best work yet is for her own company, The Learning Advantage, where she has the ability to choose her clients and colleagues. She has had her own business for 20 years! As she moved from training and organizational change to individual change, she trained to become a coach. Change at the individual level is exciting, challenging and rewarding. She has worked with over 2000 leaders to find more fulfillment in their work. That leads them to be better managers and to create workplaces where others can thrive.

Sandy is a master somatic coach, certified by the Strozzi Institute and a master coach, certified by the International Coaching Federation. She works with managers and executives to improve their leadership presence by letting their bodies talk for them in the way they intend. She understands the unique challenges leaders face in the business world, and knows the value they can bring to an organization when they have impact.

She is sought after by leaders and teams in Fortune 50 organizations, major associations, and government organizations where she has worked for over twenty years. Her expertise in individual and team coaching, organization development, and training, especially in the areas of leadership and change is well recognized and she writes and speaks frequently at major conferences on those topics.

Sandy has been married for 21 years and lives in Falls Church, VA. She and her husband enjoy travel and home projects. She loves improvisation and uses it a lot in her work. She has a hard time finding any hobbies that bring her as much joy as her work. When a client finds work that brings him alive, Sandy feels she has made a meaningful difference in the world. She wishes for everyone to have juicy work.

To learn more about *Juicy Work*, you can reach Sandy through her website at www.LearningAdvantageInc.com.

-bibliography-

Atwood, Janet and Chris. *The Passion Test.* Penguin Group, New York, NY, 2008.

Buckingham, Marcus and Curt Coffman. *First Break All The Rules-What The World's Greatest Managers Do Differently.* Simon and Schuster, New York, NY, 1999.

Buckingham, Marcus and Donald Clifton. *Now Discover Your Strengths.* The Free Press, New York, NY, 2001.

Bridges, William. *Transitions: Making Sense of Life's Changes.* Addison-Wesley, New York, NY, 1992.

Dweck, Carol. *Mindset, The New Psychology of Success.* Ballantine Books, New York, NY, 2008.

Covey, Stephen R. *The 7 Habits of Highly Effective People.* Free Press, New York, NY, 1989.

Goleman, Daniel. *Emotional Intelligence: Why It Can Matter More than IQ.* Bantam Books, New York, NY, 1995.

Leonard, George. *Mastery: The Keys to Success and Long-Term Fulfillment.* Penguin Group, New York, NY, 1992.

Mehrabian, Albert. *Silent Messages.* Wadsworth Publishing Company. 1981.

Rath, Tom. *StrengthsFinder 2.0.* Gallup Press, New York, NY, 2007.

Rath, Tom and Barry Conchie. *Strengths Based Leadership.* Gallup Press, New York, NY, 2008.

Strozzi-Heckler, Richard. *The Anatomy of Change.* North Atlantic Books, Berkeley, CA, 1984.

Strozzi-Heckler, Richard. *The Leadership Dojo.* Frog, Ltd., Berkeley, CA, 2007.

35770612R00078

Made in the USA
Charleston, SC
18 November 2014